Roger.

' Mappy Birthday' . 28.7.89.

from Mother

ν

SPITFIRE AGAINST THE ODDS

SPITFIRE AGAINST THE ODDS

R.V. ASHMAN

A William Kimber book
published by

PATRICK STEPHENS LIMITED

First published in 1989

British Library Cataloguing in Publication Data

Ashman, R. V.
Spitfire against the odds: memoirs of a
fighter pilot.
World War 2. Air operations by Great
Britain. Royal Air Force. Fighter
aeroplanes. Pilots, – Biographies
I. Title
940.54′4941′0924

ISBN 1 85260 247 3

Patrick Stephens Limited is part of the
Thorsons Publishing Group, Wellingborough,
Northamptonshire NN8 2RQ, England.

Typeset by Ann Buchan (Typesetters), Middlesex
and printed in Great Britain by
Mackays of Chatham, Kent

1 3 5 7 9 10 8 6 4 2

In remembrance of my service comrades
and in particular of the senior NCO fighter pilots of
the Royal Air Force who fought and died for their country.

Contents

Author's Note

Many historical books have been written recounting the exploits of World War II air aces over the years since 1945. This isn't one of them. With gentle persuasion I have acceded to the requests of old service friends and acquaintances to put pen to paper, to express another man's war from the other end of the scale. This factual account of my life as an ordinary airman covers the eight years of my service in the regular RAF – including the whole of the war.

All persons in this book bear their rightful names as I knew them; those I have missed out were either of no consequence or, regrettably, have been omitted owing to a failed memory. Not a diary in the strict sense of the word, it is a true narrative of my memoirs before, during, and after my service, with the help of a few technical notes, and a flying log-book.

It is not a blow by blow account of aerial fighting. I could never understand how some writers seem able to remember every single word spoken in action, every single gesture, and every single manoeuvre. I only remember vividly the moments one could not forget.

I

Early Days

High over the desert east of the Suez Canal, on one fresh, bright and sunny morning in the late autumn of 1944 I savoured a never to be forgotten moment. Here I was, the son of a working man, flying the most beautiful aeroplane in the world; it didn't seem possible; so unreal I simply could not believe it.

For the first time in many months of intensive training I had time to think about it at leisure. This was my first flight in command of a Spitfire, absolutely alone, soaring in a clear blue sky, the sun glinting on the canopy, in complete freedom; master of all I surveyed. The feeling was indescribable. Never before on a first solo flight in a strange aircraft did I feel so happy, content, and at ease, as I did with this lethal bird of prey winging along in its element. The pre-flight briefing to give one confidence, by one's battle-proven instructor, proved to be entirely unnecessary.

The aeroplane was such a delight to fly and so simple to handle, I had all the time in the world to reminisce – after throwing her all over the sky and savouring the initial, exhilarating experience of her aerobatic capabilities.

Drinking in the panoramic view of the waterways, observing the detailed contours of the sand dunes and the Arab caravans wandering along time-honoured routes towards the distant mountains in the southeast, and the main route to Palestine to the north, I found the fighter flew like a bird – so smoothly, without any effort on my part, with the unmistakable harmonious hum of the Merlin engine; so reassuring.

The flight order was: 'experience-on-type'. I had just completed an operational training course on the Hawker Hurricane. This was the next step up the ladder and the final one: conversion to the Supermarine Spitfire, before being adjudged competent enough to be a fighter pilot. This was the day I had dreamt of, ever since someone's judgement of my character nearly two years earlier had decided where my future lay – to my immense surprise and pleasure.

My thoughts went back many years meditating on how it had all come about. To be here at an Operational Flying Training School at Ismailia on the west bank of the Suez Canal training to be a fighter pilot was incredible. For the son of an engine driver, and for a time-serving airman to be a pilot *and* to be flying the crack fighter of the RAF seemed sheer fantasy.

I was born on 18 July 1920 in Oswald Terrace, Newport, on the outskirts of Middlesbrough, North Yorkshire. My father was a locomotive driver of the old North-Eastern Railway. The main line from Middlesbrough to Darlington and Newcastle ran past the bottom of our garden, behind which lay the vast mineral marshalling yards and locomotive depot of Newport. Father was based at the Middlesbrough Depot when I appeared in the world but shortly afterwards he transferred to Newport which was more convenient.

I was born a railwayman in every sense; from when I was a toddler, my whole world was centred on the railway. In 1930 – a time of depression – father made one of the most important decisions of his life when he transferred to Tweedmouth Locomotive Depot, Berwick-on-Tweed. This move was to be the biggest influence in my life. The sheds now under the control of the LNER since 1923 lay on the east coast main line from London to Edinburgh. It was to be my new world. The environment was drastically different from what I had grown accustomed to in my first ten years of life. The scenery was superlative; it had everything an adventurous boy could possibly wish for: miles of cliffs and shoreline: a beautiful unpolluted river and estuary; a historic garrison town with its King's Own Scottish Borderers Regiment stationed there; and most of all – freedom to pursue one's own interests.

My biggest regret was the absence of my younger, only brother Frank, who died of pneumonia two years earlier aged nine. We had been inseparable. He was a quiet studious lad – unlike me, the ring-leader of all the escapades we got into – sharing the subsequent inevitable punishment, without a murmur of protestation. With his demise, most of the fun in life had gone and I never quite recovered from it. A new sister took his place but she was of course ten years younger than I and a nonentity in my life. The only excitement she provided was by way of the pram. When left to ourselves, the large high pram of those days became a racing car, and after a few prangs when it went out of control, my parents had hysterics. That was the

end of my baby outings. I must say, it didn't seem to bother my
sister. I was very much alone.

Strangers were not welcome in this border town of Berwick-on-
Tweed; anyone from the south, especially, was dubbed a foreigner.
They were a very close-knit community, neither Scottish nor
English, but their antecedents were undoubtedly Scottish. They
didn't take too kindly to my father superseding the promotional
system, although it was completely out of his control and a situation
one had to accept. He had much older ex-North British Railwaymen
allocated as his firemen. I, too, suffered at school at the hands of
fellow pupils although I did my best to overcome animosity by
playing for the first eleven at cricket and taking part in athletics.
Regrettably it didn't help relations when I obviously replaced a
regular team member; magnanimous to a fault I didn't let it worry
me unduly, especially if I was instrumental in winning a few trophies
for the school.

Apart from a few close friends I gradually became a loner in my
own pursuits at Tweedmouth engine sheds where I became
well-known over the years, having gained the trust of the
railwaymen. I had *carte blanche* inside the sheds and most of the
railway complex. Father disapproved but did not prevent me. He
won over his work-mates in time, who found him a thorough
professional, tempered with thought for others. My own popularity
increased, and I made more friends than I was aware of, but I was
never fully accepted.

We occupied a lovely old cottage near Tweedmouth station and
the locomotive sheds where I was to spend most of my time over the
next seven years when I wasn't at school. One had to have a pass in
five subjects to gain the School Certificate (matriculation) in those
days – I passed in three – and the future looked grim as far as
shooting up the ladder in my chosen career of steam mechanical
engineering was concerned. One had to possess the School
Certificate to gain access to a University unless one's parents were
wealthy.

The only remaining opportunity left open was to start work at the
age of 18 as a locomotive cleaner, the first rung of the ladder to
becoming a driver and the dizzy heights of a locomotive inspector.
But it was still possible with my advanced technical knowledge to
circumvent the system to promote myself more rapidly. Taking odd
jobs, I waited until I was 18, and was put on the first substantive

rung on the ladder as a locomotive-cleaner – then immediately laid off before I had even started. My brand new overalls were returned to the store.

Another economic depression had raised its ugly head practically overnight and the shedmaster told me as a friend to forget the railway; there would be no opportunities of a career with them in the foreseeable future. If there had been the slightest chance, I knew he would have tipped me off. It was a deadly blow to my aspirations – I never quite got over it. I was bitterly disappointed that I had worked so hard for eight years without result and was never to work with the steam engines I loved. I had to disentangle my mind and try to readjust to a new life. Quite what – I had no idea.

Speed in any sphere thrilled me; it led to many admonitions in my school days from the headmaster and the constabulary for repeatedly recklessly riding a small bicycle – with my chum Dickson on the crossbar – at an excessive speed down the steep High Street on our way from school and taking the corner on to the Tweed Bridge at a hairy angle. I first drove a van under age on the public highway; it was more than a year later when I was caught by a local bobby.

Time waits for no man they say. There was this little twit called Hitler making a nuisance of himself and he had marched into Austria during March 1938. There seemed to be a bit of a flap on about Czechoslovakia and a tiny piece of it called Sudetenland which looked as though it was going to upset all the politicians when he decided he wanted that too. There was an atmosphere of urgency, excitement and rumours of war. At the end of July – my birthday was the 18th – I knew I had no future with the railway. On the rebound, inspired by the speed record-breaking feat of the new Hawker Hurricane from London to Edinburgh and a sudden recruitment drive by the Royal Air Force with a lot of flag waving and propaganda, I gave some serious thought to enlisting.

There was nothing for me at home. I came to the conclusion I might have something to offer the Royal Air Force. On making enquiries from this famous service at the Newcastle Recruitment Centre, it appeared that I was just the type they were looking for. My biggest mistake was being too young and too unworldly to ask the pertinent questions that would have done *me* the most good, rather than the RAF. Consequently I was given the full cajoling, bullshine treatment by the officer-in-charge. I was educated above the standard required and would have no trouble in choosing a service

career to my liking – how naive could one be. One only had to pass
the entrance examination, be declared medically fit and the world
was one's oyster. They would provide every opportunity for me to
succeed in whatever branch I chose. No one told me that a new flying
branch was now available under the new RAF Extension scheme.

On 16 August 1938, I left home to see the world, which started at
West Drayton near London, where I signed on for seven years'
regular service and five in the Reserve. It was a traumatic fortnight
for me away from home, wondering if I had done the right thing and
reflecting once again on my early dreams and ruined career.

However, I was looking forward to what I thought was going to be
a new, exciting adventure – and a bright new future in the best
service in the world – or so the officer commanding told us. I believed
him. What I found hard to understand was that although numerous
trades were mentioned, whenever I asked about them they had a
habit of saying not to worry, it will all be sorted out later! Finally, I
nailed a corporal down and asked him what future there was for me,
he said, 'You will go where you are told', and much more, I can't
repeat here. Asked about flying, he laughed. 'You must be joking,
only officers and pigs might fly.' Had I made a mistake? When a
large party of recruits eventually enlisted, we were escorted to RAF
Station Cardington, Bedfordshire for what they called basic training
but which turned out to be two months of 'square bashing' – nothing
but drill and physical training in charge of Royal Marine and
Guardsmen instructors seconded to the RAF for the express purpose
of making our lives a misery, or so it seemed to us. We were kitted out
originally with pantaloons and bindings with the old army style
tunic and shirts that were collarless and guaranteed to take one's
skin off if they came in contact with it. However, the uniform was
temporary owing to the quartermaster stores being empty of trousers
and the sudden large influx of recruits. We were glad to part with the
pantaloons for ordinary trousers when they arrived. Why pantaloons
were adopted by the Royal Flying Corps in the first place is a
mystery; it took hours to wind the puttees on correctly, only to find
one couldn't walk let alone march. When the weather was inclement,
the vast hangar that once housed the huge airships R100 and R101
which came to a disastrous end in France on its maiden voyage to
India on 5 October 1930, was quite large enough to facilitate drilling
hundreds of recruits at one time, so there was no let-up in the order of
things. Once again recruits were confined to camp but this time for a

month. After a month we didn't recognize ourselves. We were a different breed of men; one that the RAF could take pride in, by allowing the general public to see us.

We were issued with silver RAF-crest topped swagger canes, and peaked hats. Forage caps were not allowed to be worn, and needless to say, everyone was inspected before setting foot outside the camp. We were up to Guards' standard and were forced to uphold it by the numerous RAF police patrols in Bedford, which was the only town that had cinemas but very little else unless one was a drinker. Most of us, including myself, didn't imbibe in those days – on 12 shillings a fortnight it was out of the question anyway. Out of that we made an allowance to our parents as insurance, and in case of death, they received an RAF pension.

Towards the end of training, we spent hours on the shooting range firing the Lee Enfield .303 rifle with real ammunition. I took to this like a duck to water; one of the most enjoyable pursuits we had. I was turned out as a good marksman after the initial shocks of mastering the recoil and sore shoulder. The more practice we had the better and even the instructors said I should take it up as a sport. It was very relaxing out on the range and one felt it was a sport rather than a means of killing someone. Not that we in the RAF were ever expected to do that. Most of our leisure time was spent in our huts boning up boots until one could see his face in them; blancoing our belts and equipment; cleaning rifles and polishing bayonet sheaths and of course all the brasses on uniforms and equipment. This had to be done every night! The hutments had to be spotless even to black-leading the heating stove, whitewashing its base and polishing the floor by hand. When 'lights out' sounded, everybody was in bed, absolutely fatigued.

I didn't realise it at the time, but I had been unfortunate to join when the Government had decided to expand the RAF, owing to the sabre-rattling of Hitler. Hence the huge numbers of recruits and seconded Army and Marine NCOs and the lack of interest of Regular Officers over what to do with us. We were (ACH GD) Aircrafthand General Duties category with the lowest rank of (AC2) Aircraftman Class 2, and more fitted for the Marines than the Air Force with our training. Tradesmen in the RAF (engine/airframe fitters, electricians, wireless operators, wireless electrical mechanics, etc.) were all boy entrants or apprentices from the ages of 14 and 16 respectively. So little was left for the rest of us, despite the publicity and assurances made by recruiting officers and devious methods used by the RAF to attract young men to the service. It was nothing less than a confidence trick. A number of recruits had already bought themselves out, thoroughly disillusioned, and there was still time (three months) to follow suit. The problem was that it was so very expensive. I was determined not to return home with my tail between my legs even if my parents could afford it. I knew I would never live it down in the community of Berwick-on-Tweed. I had to prove to the world and myself that I could take adversity in my stride. Ironically the recession was to come to an end a year hence on the railway and I could have been gainfully employed in the work that had been my life-time dream.

The thought of spending the next seven years as a nonentity was simply appalling. If there was to be no future for me in the RAF, believe me, the next boat for China would have found a stowaway shipped aboard. I always had a love for the sea and ships, second only to railways and steam locomotives. Adventure was the spice of life to me. I would tackle anything that presented a challenge. I could not tolerate a mundane existence but blessed with stoical characteristics, I knew I would win one day, no matter how long it took. I would overcome all the obstacles placed in my way and however rough the going was, I would show the RAF and everyone else that I was not a quitter. Consequently my passage through the RAF was anything but smooth. It was against all the odds that I set out to prove myself.

*

I was summoned to an interview with the Chief Administrative Officer at which he gave me the news that he was remustering me to clerk and posting me to RAF Grantham where No. 12 Flying Training School was to be formed. I was to be transferred to the Signals (W/T) Section; he was sure the signals officer would give me sympathetic consideration. Feeling elated I packed my kit-bag and left for RAF Station Spitalgate, Grantham on 28 October 1938. At last I was to be stationed on a real RAF aerodrome with, I hoped, a more exciting life.

The atmosphere on entering the gates was entirely different from what had gone before. I was a source of amusement with my short back-and-sides hair-cut from the moment I reported to the guard-room; an obvious rooky, jumping about like an automaton, brain-washed into obeying commands from a LAC (leading aircraftman) in the guardroom who had no authority whatsoever; but I wasn't aware of that. I was told, amid howls of mirth, by the guard commander that the LAC was on jankers (under punishment), and he was a prisoner cleaning the cells out! When I got to know this character later we couldn't stop laughing at my ignorance, but I did feel a fool. There were many such incidents as I began to learn about the devious, cunning and mischievous life of the lowly airman. However, I was put at ease by the corporal-in-charge of the RAF Police, and he shepherded me to the station headquarters leaving me in the care of an orderly.

I was marched to my first encounter with the SWO (Station Warrant Officer). On my arrival at HQ, he examined the sealed documents I presented and his orderly allocated me a bed in one of the brick barrack rooms with central heating and bathrooms! After a short walk around the station and the hangars, observing more people in overalls (boiler suits) than in uniforms, I began to feel I really was in the Royal Air Force.

RAF Station Spitalgate (Grantham) was an old airfield dating back to the first war, opened in 1916 with a collection of wooden huts. It was situated on top of a hill two miles south of the town of Grantham.

On my arrival No 106 (Fairey Battle) Battle Squadron was preparing to leave. The station was static for a few weeks until No 12 Service Flying Training School was formed. The hangars had an intoxicating aroma of dope and grease, and a few lovely silver Hawker biplanes; the first operational aircraft I had ever seen. Discipline was obviously maintained, though much more casually in the workshops. In fact I felt out of place in my spotless new uniform. The airfield was all grass with tarmac aprons and parking lots: there was little activity but one felt the atmosphere. There was an indefinable air about the place. Quite relaxing.

My feeling of contentment wasn't to last very long for me when I reported back to the SWO. He said that he was sending me on a fire-fighter course and when I protested that I was a clerk posted to the Signals Section (wireless telegraphy transmitting and receiving station), he said that the remuster had not been promulgated. This meant that it had not been authorised by Air Ministry Records yet; it was only a recommendation from the OC (Officer Commanding) Cardington, and had to be ratified.

Waiting for this fire-fighting course I was given the usual onerous domestic general duties of cleaning lavatories, painting boundary stones white, polishing floors, sweeping the small parade ground, kitchen fatigues and all the dirty duties the SWO could find to keep his men occupied.

Needless to say, I received a new education from the hardened general duties mob who had everything taped to a nicety and against my nature I learnt the art – believe me it really was an art – of dodging the column or skiving. It was made more difficult because the SWO and his underlings had all done it in their early days, so one had to outwit the experts. Dodging the column and skiving were of course, malingering and making oneself scarce when some obnoxious job was in the offing.

The day arrived when I was sent to Cranwell for a short fire-fighting course. On my return to Grantham I was moved to the Fire Station's sleeping quarters, with a Sergeant-in-Charge. He was a pleasant, red-haired chap, with a relaxed manner. The section consisted of only six full-time firemen, the numbers were made up to 16 by fire-pickets detailed off their normal duties in the event of a fire.

The most responsible duties were on the crash-tender, standing at readiness on the tarmac in front of the control tower.

During my service on the crash-tender, however, I received a fractured femur in the summer of 1939, when clambering up the access steps on the back of the tender to check the pressure of the foam containers. I was a guinea pig for a new treatment for fractured femurs but I had implicit faith in the Group Captain Surgeon who operated. Three years later he wrote to me to ask how my leg was bearing up and if I was having any trouble with it. If so, I had to let him know and he would have me recalled to hospital. At that time it was common to be left with the fractured leg shorter than the other, but after the treatment I received, both legs were of the same length. I was full of admiration for their devoted service.

It may have done me a good turn involuntarily. I learnt I was now transferred to the Signals Section to be trained as a teleprinter operator with three other chaps. The section had expanded with the flying school coming on stream and with the outbreak of war; they now had responsibility for maintaining 24-hour wireless communications with Air Ministry and bomber group headquarters in the vicinity. Later an RDF (radio direction finding) station was erected nearby and operators from the camp were called upon to man them. Not content with attaining a speed of 60 words per minute on the teleprinter and remustering to a T/P Op and taking control of the landline sub-section, I sat with the wireless operators receiving cypher messages by morse sent on the regular hourly Air Ministry broadcasts to all stations, until I was proficient enough to read the code at the normal 20 words per minute. Three of the five T/P Ops including myself were recommended for a wireless operators' training course.

On the outbreak of war, barbed wire was erected around the airfield and we had the forerunners of the Home Guard making themselves apparent in the shape of patriotic elderly chaps, mostly ex-soldiers of the Great War, who reported in the evenings for training on rifle drill, using the old American Ross single-shot rifles. They patrolled the perimeters of the airfield and became more of a menace to us than the enemy. Until their arrival we had slipped out of the camp through the hedges when for some reason we were confined to camp and the guard-room wouldn't issue a pass-out, returning the same way.

I was promoted to AC1, (Aircraftman first class) no longer a rookie. Experienced, established wireless operators were now being urged to remuster to W/Op-AG (Wireless Operator/Air Gunners). The fatality rate was appalling in the period of late 1939 and 1940. The lifespan of air gunners was very short, flying in such early bombers as Hampdens, Whitleys and Battles, all of them death traps, under-powered, under-gunned, and entirely outclassed by the German defences. The category of AG (Air Gunner) became a full-time trade in January 1939 when they were given the rank of sergeant, and issued with the cloth half-wing brevet for the first time. This was the so-called silly season. The introduction of the Wellington bombers and the expansion of Bomber Command required more AGs and subsequently more losses to be replaced as activity increased.

Inevitably, sound, good men, masters of their trade, couldn't resist the chance of immediate promotion to sergeant, or felt they couldn't sit back in the country's hour of need and so volunteered to fly, one of the tragic aspects of the war. The Air Ministry in their pedantic preparations for the war never allowed for the huge loss of life of skilled men not intended for flying duties in peacetime.

I was granted an interview with the Chief Administrative Officer (adjutant) to ask him if my name could be put forward for aircrew training. Certainly he said, we need air gunners very badly. I told him that I wanted to take part in actually flying the aircraft as a pilot or to navigate it. Not that I didn't admire the rest of the crew, but I felt I wanted to be in a position of responsibility for the aircraft. He was very affable but he said that I should have applied as a direct entry, when I would have been adjudged suitable material or not.

He appeared to be amused at the very idea that I thought I was good enough for consideration for anything other than a rear air gunner, whose lifespan at that time was two or three weeks. He said that he understood that I was waiting to change my trade to wireless operator and my speed of receiving morse was first class at 25 words per minute, so perhaps I should reapply later as a W/Op air gunner. There was little future in it but I told him I would give it some thought as soon as I was a wireless operator.

However, an extremely lucky quirk of fate was to intervene at this fortuitous moment. My destiny was about to change completely, much to my amazement, but not without the pitfalls that seemed to dog every step I took.

II

The Path to the Cockpit

The quirk of fate was a young flight lieutenant education officer posted to Grantham during 1941. He was a donnish figure who had suffered disappointment from the appointments board when they turned down his application for a flying career on the grounds that he was too academically qualified and the RAF required his services in the classroom. A man of his calibre should have commanded a better post than a lecturer at 12 SFTS in addition to all the flying and ground instructors. With the lack of social activities due to the awkward watch-keeping hours I borrowed books from him and did some serious tutorial work in the winter months. He formed a nucleus of students among the airmen in their spare time. I let my hair down as it were, bringing him up to date with my career and the interview with the adjutant. After an examination of my academic work, he said he could see no reason why a flying career wasn't within my grasp if I did a little more work. Taking his advice and tuition I eventually passed the equivalent of the GCE and he submitted his recommendations to the Aircrew Selection Board.

It wasn't until early 1942 that I received orders to attend an Aircrew Selection Board at Padgate (Manchester). With some trepidation I presented myself. The Board consisted of five members and was chaired by an Air Vice-Marshal. My head was as clear as a bell when I was ushered into the presence of this august body, paying them due reverence. There were two members of the Board I felt I had an affinity with, one a wing commander and the other a group captain. They were nevertheless very astute in their questioning. Fortunately I scored with my past record and on technical matters in which the wing commander was well versed, and I played in the Groupie's eleven as wicket-keeper in 1939 in an Inter-Command Cricket Trophy game at Chelmsford, which we won; surprisingly he never forgot it. He remarked to the rest, 'Good cricketer, this chap.' It gave me a warm feeling but quite what it had to do with the business of selecting a future flier I've no idea.

The rest of the Board asked the usual questions, e.g. what was your father's profession: what school did you attend: why at this late stage do you want to fly. Of course I was honest to a degree even to telling the chairman that the Royal Air Force hadn't given me, and others like me, any opportunity to do so previously.

I left Padgate for Grantham feeling as the other candidates did, that I had blown it. The usual class-ridden questions of what your father did and what school did one attend sickened me. The wing commander was on my side, emphasizing the resolute efforts I had made for the betterment of my career in the service and showing the tenacity the service required. The other two group captains were more concerned about whether I was officer material; on that score I knew I had no chance – not when my father was an engine driver! They belonged to the old staff officer brigade.

It struck me as being extremely odd in 1940 that during the Battle of Britain the RAF was crying out for pilots. They had plenty of aircraft but too few pilots to fly them. Yet if the Air Ministry hadn't been so class-ridden they had a vast reserve. The pupil pilots of 12 SFTS carried the rank of sergeant until they received their Wings and were commissioned.

Throughout my service life I had been led to believe that other ranks had virtually no chance of becoming a pilot, unless one was accepted as such before joining the service and considered as officer material. As a consequence it never occurred to anyone that it was possible, provided they could fend off discouragement from the service hierarchy.

Later in 1940 the system was changed. Pupils were now aircrew cadets; saving money no doubt by giving the Air Council breathing space to decide who should grace the officers' mess and who were undesirable. It was fairly obvious they were extremely reluctant to acknowledge the value of the sergeant pilots in the Battle of Britain, but they would have been in a sorry state without them. Commissions depended upon who you were and what college you attended. It made them officers but not necessarily gentlemen, but what was more to the point; it had no bearing on their skill as pilots. Senior NCO pilots had the authority of their rank, but they were discouraged from using it by administrative and disciplinarian officers. They were supposed to be above that sort of thing and only carried the rank of sergeant and above for protection from the lower ranks – similar to the RAF Police – with some small privilege accorded them by the enemy if they were unlucky to be shot down. Needless to say, the ground NCOs didn't integrate with the NCO pilots. There was a certain amount of resentment and jealousy on their part. The system was farcical; pilots carried temporary rank, never substantive; it could be taken away at any time, and was, when one was grounded permanently on any pretext, especially medical.

This could never apply to an officer doing exactly the same job. In Bomber Command a sergeant was expected to risk his life in a bomber in a mixed crew, but deemed not worthy enough to use the officers' mess, and it should never be forgotten that all aircrew were volunteers. This Command had the sense to turn a blind eye on occasion when officers and men of a bomber crew fraternised at parties and in the local pubs, although it was strictly forbidden.

A signal eventually arrived from Air Ministry in the summer of 1942, like a bolt out of the blue. I had no great expectations of passing that Selection Board. I was resigned to the fact that I wasn't wanted for flying. I seldom read the Daily Routine Orders (DRO) and when one of the wags dashed in the telegraph room and told me we had a budding navigator on the staff, I thought he was taking the mickey. I allowed myself to be frog-marched to the notice board and there it was in black and white. I couldn't believe it; my luck had changed. I was going to fly – absolutely incredible. Six months waiting and there it was: 'LAC R.V. Ashman from this date is remustered to LAC U/T Navigator (Navigator-under-training)'.

Unfortunately another later-dated AMO remustered me again, but this time to AC1 W/T Operator. That really put the cat among the pigeons and stirred my superiors into a fever of activity. At this stage I needed all my wits about me. I wouldn't allow anything to stand in the way of my becoming a navigator; otherwise I would be a wireless operator for the rest of my service and probably sent to some god-forsaken overseas outpost if I resisted pressure to fly as a wireless operator air gunner.

Station HQ and the Signals Officer disregarded the signals, telling me they had been referred back to Records. I ignored them and inserted the white flash in a fold of my cap signifying I was an aircrew cadet. The ultimate conclusion of this bizarre situation came when a movement order was received from Air Ministry Records to post one senior teleprinter operator to Air Ministry Communications Centre, Leighton Buzzard. The golden opportunity to get rid of me presented itself. Regardless of my protestations that I was no longer under the jurisdiction of Station HQ and I was now a wireless operator anyway, I was listed to be posted with the rank of acting corporal on 9 November 1942. If commonsense had prevailed, my status would have been referred back with some urgency to AM Records and confirmation received, but nobody could care less. I was out on a limb.

We had a glorious farewell party on the eve of my departure. The whole wireless section and all my friends on the station had chipped in to make my last night a memorable one. With an uncanny instinct, mates who were on duty also found time to drop in in the course of it.

Apart from possibly a few instructor junior NCOs at the schools, I was one of the first teleprinter operators to be promoted to acting-corporal, but that would be the end of promotional prospects in this trade for males. The Women's Auxiliary Air Force were taking over in the United Kingdom.

*

It was a very dejected, lonely figure that arrived at Leighton Buzzard, weighed down with two kit-bags and full marching order equipment, not to mention the biggest hangover I'd ever had. It was a small agricultural town those days, on the fringe of the green belt, 15 miles from London.

Air Ministry Signals was a vast underground network in solid concrete which I took a dislike to immediately. I thought I was on another planet when I was escorted through a maze of tunnels to meet the Signals Officer to report for duty. He was a commissioned officer, a flight lieutenant responsible to the Chief Communications Officer. He was purely administrative and left most of the work to his warrant officer and subordinates. It was peculiar to the communications branch in the RAF, that commissioned signals officers generally had no qualifications applicable to the trade. Nobody had ever met an officer who knew the first principles of wireless-telegraphy let alone how to use a trans-receiver. Telecommunications was a comparatively new trade set up by the boffins and W/T was on its way out overland. Hence the increasing numbers of WAAF teleprinter operators. The RAF relied on W/T NCOs for the efficient running of the Centre. The maintenance of the equipment was in the hands of civilians employed by the GPO.

I could not help noticing on my arrival in the small town the colossal numbers of WAAFs milling around; there were hundreds of them! At Grantham we had less than a dozen in the whole area and none in the signals section. It gave me an insecure feeling to see all these females around – let me hasten to add not an unpleasant one. The sight of so many well proportioned legs and figures lifted one's morale no end, and so much of it everywhere one looked. One's mind immediately sensed that one couldn't go wrong in such a situation, especially feeling lost and in need of mothering when one's morale was so low. . .

This euphoria wasn't to last, unfortunately, particularly when I found I was billeted in an old barn!

Reporting for my first duty down in the bowels of the earth, I discovered I was NCO-in-Charge of a watch. A watch was a certain number of people on duty for a certain length of time before they were relieved by the next one to follow – mine, consisted of 80 WAAF teleprinter operators! Operational orders were received over the teleprinter-links during the day from Bomber and Coastal Command Headquarters, which originated at Whitehall and Churchill's bunker. In the evening these highly secret orders were disseminated throughout the huge transmitting room which contained hundreds of teleprinters, switchboards, automatic perforators and transmitters. According to the designation, the signals were distributed to various sections for onward transmission to various operational commands telling them what their targets were that night. Needless to say, the time factor was cut to the bare minimum from the time of origination to the time the groups and squadrons received the orders. It was exacting work for all concerned; with very little rest whilst on duty.

My next posting was to Horsham St Faith, Norwich, to take charge of the Signals section under the command of the 8th USAAF. The Americans had recently arrived in this country with the van of their bombers, establishing a base at Horsham St Faith which had for many years been an RAF base. They brought Boston medium-bombers, taking quite some time to work up to operational strength and efficiency.

The base was now to all intents and purposes American, guarded by them and run administratively by them. The only RAF outpost was the Signals section manned by RAF teleprinter operators only. I had a feeling that AM was trying to write me off.

In January 1943 I was recalled to Leighton after handing over the Signals Section to our equivalent American communications personnel who had just got off the boat. The colonel thanked us for our 'invaluable' services and laid on a small reception for us in an ante-room of the officers' mess, where we were wined and dined and a little overawed.

On reporting to the hierarchy I was told I was remustered to wireless operator, and reclassified as AC2. This meant I was reduced from a corporal back to the lowest classification in the RAF as a recruit, but with the trade of W/T Op. Worse still, I was demoted from my proper grade of three years as leading aircraftman to the lowest one, because of the change of trade. Fate once again had dealt me an unjust, cruel blow.

So after nearly four-and-a-half years' service I had attained what I set out to do at the expense of losing three years' service in a higher paid grade. It would take me another three years to attain my rank with the wireless-op badge on my arm. Whilst I was wondering what action I could take, if any, the signals officer received a posting order, to wit: post one wireless operator to the Middle East. You guessed, AC2 R.V. Ashman was elected and proffered to the Movements Officer Records.

There comes a time in everyone's life I suppose, when having given the problem a great deal of thought with a crucial decision to make, one must take the bull by the horns for better or worse. After a week of waiting the order came through telling me to report to a Personnel Disposal Centre at Manchester, where I would be kitted out in tropical kit for the HQ Middle East Command (Cairo). In the meantime I pressed my claim again, as an aircrew cadet under-training. The Signals HQ staff didn't want to know about it, so when the posting order arrived, I simply refused to go!

Yes, I flatly refused. I was not of a rebellious nature. I prided myself on my integrity, and had been commended on more than one occasion for devotion to duty. Now I threw caution to the winds and didn't care a damn about anything or anyone.

I decided I would go for broke, and told the Signals Officer that I would not leave on any boat, until the circumstances had been properly investigated. I was put in cells for failing to carry out a lawful command.

The Station Commander restored my faith in the service by his searching enquiries, bringing to light the glowing report on me from the US 8th Army Air Force of which he was unaware; confirming my status from the AVM, Chairman of the Aircrew Selection Board and investigated the ostensible excuses of the senior NCOs of the section. Morale soared; I was ecstatic. My character had won through and my past record was recognised as impeccable. Luckily the CO had an instinct for the truth which makes itself apparent if one is resolute enough. He knew by experience and, if I may use a colloquialism, he knew I wasn't pulling a fast one. I also thanked God for the power and the influence of the Aircrew Selection Board.

Who would have thought that such gargantuan efforts would have to be made by an ordinary airman in his efforts to volunteer to fly and fight for his country! But they were, believe me.

*

The serious business of air-navigation commenced in March at No 8 ITW in Newquay, Cornwall. This was a mixed course of 50 pupil pilots and navigators but everyone had to undergo the ground training academically and physically. To me it was ecstasy. I loved the environment and the long distance running before breakfast; I was extremely fit; athletics were no problem to me and I thoroughly enjoyed it. Academic work was absorbing; we had to learn the theory of flight from the very beginning among other subjects, and I loved it. It will be gathered by now that I liked challenges, so what could be better? We went swimming, practising survival at sea after ditching and in general had a glorious time in that beautifully hot summer on those wide, long stretches of silvery sands.

Unfortunately, only 39 candidates passed for further training. One could fail on any one subject, and it was irrevocable. We had the usual passing out parade and the festivities that night, which lasted until dawn. The failures wished us luck and faded away. I felt terribly upset that some of them were not coming with us, some of the nicest chaps one could wish to live and work with. We were not aware of it then, but the Allies were beginning to win the air war, with the advent of larger, better defended bombers and more successful night-raid tactics. The conduct of the war had changed and the RAF were cutting down the numbers of pupils for further training; only the most successful would accomplish their dreams of flying. A large reserve had been built up, but 1944 dissipated them very quickly in Bomber Command which makes the following events incongruous.

The course finished at the end of July. We were all to be posted to Heaton Park, Manchester; an aircrew departure centre for advanced schools. The CO said that we were going for some flying at Sywell before going there, filling in time and cutting down the length of stay at Manchester. I had nothing to lose; I was to go on an advanced navigator's course somewhere, so I jumped at the chance of a pleasant few days in the countryside.

At Sywell they were flying Tiger Moth dual bi-planes. I was told to get in the rear cockpit and the instructor climbed in the front. I thought I was in for a few days of flying experience, air-sickness test, and cruising around observing the landscape and putting my navigational training to good use. But much to my surprise, the instructor handed over the controls after we had taken off and told me to fly it. I'd received no tuition whatever, except from what I had learnt in a boy's magazine. After a run through the procedure I did; banking to the left and then to the right with a careful eye on the turn-and-bank indicator, keeping it steady with no skid, I settled down and began to enjoy this thrillingly new adventure.

In no time at all I could take off and land and do some aerobatics. It was a marvellous experience which I would not have missed for the world. Unfortunately the instructor said I was limited to 14 flying hours. So that was the end of a short but invigorating interlude. Some of my fellow students from Newquay who were pilots-under-training did exceedingly well going solo after five hours flying. I congratulated them on this remarkable achievement with the thought that they at least had nothing further to worry about. I was quite happy about my own future, but actually flying an aircraft was a very exciting experience, although I didn't solo – my landings were not good enough it would seem to risk sending me off on my own – but I would never forget it for the rest of my life.

The day of days for me was 10 September 1943. We had paraded as usual when I heard: '6........ LAC Ashman.'

'Sir,' I answered.

'You are remustered to pilot-under-training'.

It took me some time to get over the shock, I simply could not believe it, I was sure they had made a mistake. I was astounded, it was so incredible! Some of the chaps that flew at Sywell, fellow students at ITW, and good enough to solo in five hours, were down-graded to bomb-aimers or taken out of the training scheme altogether!

I could not contain my feelings. To say I was overjoyed was to put it mildly. I could not express my feelings adequately. I was so ecstatic and honoured. It was beyond my wildest dreams to have the opportunity of training to fly an aeroplane, a captain; I would not have swopped it for a knighthood. The pilot's role was so much more adventurous and exciting from take-off to landing. Who could wish for more?

The next move wasn't long coming. We were all aboard a night train heading north, through Dumfries and after some shunting in the Clyde we arrived at Greenock, to board the *Windsor Castle*, a Union-Castle liner en route for South Africa.

III

Airborne at Last

No 6 Air School Potchefstroom was about 30 miles south-west of Johannesburg, and miles away from town or any habitation. To the west stretched the Kalahari Desert, undulating, scrubland; stock farming reached northwards to Bechuanaland, and the veldt covered with kopjes (hills) ran south with the river; eastwards lay the mines of the 'Rand' and Johannesburg. The airfield was one large flat area with little grass growing on it; a hard bumpy surface. We were isolated, well away from any populace. The weather was glorious. In the heat of the South African summer the biggest danger to everyone was the terrific thunderstorms that built up by the searing midday sun. The ground level at nearly 4,000 feet above sea-level wasn't particularly noticeable until taking-off and landing; it had the effect of making take-off runs longer and landings much shorter. Our flight was equally divided between South African pupils and RAF pupils, numbering 50 in total under Captain R.F. Roberts, South African Air Force, Officer Commanding. The instructors were a mixture of SAAF and RAF pilots. My instructor was a paragon of flying and a gifted teacher. He had gained his wings out there but wasn't allowed to further his operational ambitions; he was one of the chosen few retained as an instructor.

He was Pilot Officer G.H. Godkin, about the same age as myself, if not a year or two younger. He was a smashing chap to get on with, one of the boys, no side, but a really zealous instructor, who would stand no nonsense in the air. We, and I mean the 25 RAF pupils, thought the South African pupils and staff strange at first; they were undoubtedly different to us in their philosophy. Well-built, hardened to the climate, they looked older than they were. They were all officer cadets, there were no NCO pilots in the SAAF, and they were inclined to be stand-offish. Of course they had no experience of wartime out there, so I believe they were covering up some inferiority complex, added to the fact that they had the choice when they gained their wings of becoming involved in our war or remaining at home. A choice most of us didn't have or want, otherwise we wouldn't be there.

The difference in the system out there was that the SAAF pupils were first and foremost officers, whereas the RAF pupils were first and foremost pilot material. The effect of this will be apparent later when a summary of successful candidates disclosed the inconsistencies of both systems. It was all down to an attitude of mind. Did one want to succeed in order to fight a war or not, irregardless of rank? There *was* a choice.

Nevertheless we had to rub shoulders with the SAAF pupils and apart from a few patriotic chaps who had British blood in their veins they kept themselves aloof. We had more than enough work to occupy ourselves with to worry about the different factions; we had a job to do and we were scared to death we weren't up to it. The thought of being scrubbed and sent home gave us the willies in moments of despair. As mentioned previously, the ground level already 3,000 ft and more above sea level meant that when flying at 2,000 ft on one's altimeter, the Moth was actually 5,000 ft and flying just below its maximum ceiling height. It put a great strain on the small 130hp engine with a top speed of 109 mph at 1,000 ft, considerably reduced the higher she climbed, and made control just that little bit more difficult for the pilot, due to the thinner air.

My problem was landing. I had already flown 14 hours in England as you will recall, without going solo. I knew I had to do it within five hours here and I felt the pressure. The instructor could not fault my general flying including aerobatics, recovery from spinning and stalling etc. but making a three-point landing (two undercarriage wheels and tail skid simultaneously) was a problem. Engine-powered landings on two wheels were easy, but I had great difficulty in stalling the aircraft two feet from the ground with the engine dead. The Tiger Moth was a lovely little aeroplane to fly, extremely light to handle; it bounced around the sky like a feather and had the same attributes when landing – which was the draw-back.

Poor Godkin was worried; he couldn't understand it, we had mastered every manoeuvre in the book, a progress test by Captain Roberts after five hours was very favourable but he wouldn't consent to my first solo trip. It was decided through the pleadings of my instructor that I would be given a little extra time, concentrating on the 'glide approach and landing' manoeuvre. Captain Roberts gave me another test on 6 January 1944 and finally he climbed out of the aircraft, took the 'stick' out of the front cockpit and fastened the harness together and said, 'She is all yours and the best of luck.' I will never forget that episode. I hadn't done a particularly good landing with him so it was a complete surprise to be told to go solo. It was neck or nothing now.

Suddenly far from being nervous I was elated. Taxying out to the boundary to turn into wind and taking off was the most exciting thing that had ever happened to me, she took off like a bird, climbing to 1,000 feet and turning left to circle the airfield – it seemed odd with nobody sitting in the front seat but the realisation I was completely alone only enhanced the exhilarating pleasure of flying the machine. Flying according to the book, turning correctly with an eye on the instruments in a square circuit back to the downward leg, I thought about the landing, but I knew instinctively I was going to do it first time without having to go round again as so many other chaps had been forced to do. I turned across wind, throttling back and losing height, turned into wind, throttle closed, eased back on the stick keeping straight with the rudder she glided in and made a beautiful three-point landing and stuck to the ground. I saw Captain Roberts and Pilot Officer Godkin hiding behind a hut, but as I taxied in they rushed out to congratulate me, more pleased than I was.

Needless to say, that night a certain person strutted around the mess as though he owned it, with jocular remarks coming from his friends such as 'Don't tell us you made it at last; we thought you were a penguin.'

The ten minute flight sealed my future, I felt like an ace already, but the next day I was brought down to earth by Godkin on our dual flights by more critical and pressurised instruction. Naturally I was sent off more and more on solo flights to practise by myself what I had learnt with him and found myself in quite a number of predicaments that gradually disappeared with experience. It was said that if one could fly a Tiger Moth, one could fly anything. She was a simple machine with very little power, as fast as a speedy family car – but that was where the skill or lack of it made itself apparent. She was so gentle and light one had to work hard to fly her; a simple roll was one of the hardest manoeuvres to accomplish with perfection, entailing exact co-ordination of hand and feet. A loop was accomplished by putting the nose down with full throttle, pulling back on the stick tightly until inverted, throttle closed – the fuel ceased to flow into the carburettor upside down being gravitationally fed – gently easing the stick forward to prevent stalling as she curved downwards towards earth and opening the throttle as one flattened out. Otherwise the engine had a habit of cutting out as she came out of the loop. Of course a roll off the top of a loop was harder still with no engine, inverted and little forward speed. Nevertheless she was a lovely unsophisticated tiny machine, subjected to every small air current, equipped with less dials than a car, one control column, a rudder bar, a small throttle lever, turn and bank indicator and a compass. The weather conditions and terrain over which we flew accentuated the little tricks of the aircraft and made better pilots of us. Underneath a large cumulo-nimbus cloud the little machine could be sucked up hundreds of feet or dropped without warning, sometimes upside down. One either recovered control quickly or one cashed in one's chips. It was forbidden to fly intentionally through these huge clouds after one aircraft had its wing torn off in a particularly bad storm, losing the instructor and his pupil. The little moth was only canvas and wood and held together by wires and struts.

Flying straight and level at low altitude over the veldt was impossible for the hot currents of air rising from the ground to be replaced by cold currents from above created much turbulence. Formation flying was one of the very last exercises at the end of the course, at a height considered safe to do so. The RAF expression 'bumpy conditions' was with us here all the time except early morning, bouncing around like a butterfly.

I found the country fascinating in many ways, there were the strange names of townships we flew to, or over, such as Losberg, Vredefort, Kroonstad, Parys and other unpronounceable names; the barren hills and dried up river beds and valleys south of our base: the winding railway lines threading their way over the veldt and through the valleys – conspicuous by the lack of them – knowing that one single line probably stretched for hundreds of miles between depots as they called the stations. They came in very useful on cross-country navigation flights. If one was lost in the constant haze that pervaded the landscape during daytime, one looked for a railway line, generally the Cape to Salisbury line and flew down it until a wayside station appeared. Having pinpointed one's position it was easy to map read and set a compass course for the ultimate destination. Similarly the river Mooi was the only river large enough to be continuously flowing; consequently it saved many lost pilots when they saw the gleam of water and worked out their position from a peculiar bend in the river. On the other hand if a chap was completely lost and had to either bale out or force land in some dreadful terrain, his chances of survival were slim; communities were spread so far apart, he would never make it on his own if he was injured. A bell was rung when a pupil was missing on a cross-country exercise, and all available aircraft took off over the preplanned course he should have flown, fanning out on each side to search every donga (eroded watercourse) and kopje. It was important to find the missing flier before dark. The veldt was crawling with snakes, tarantulas and scorpions and a few small wild animals but not the large species of course, which had been driven west to the desert regions. Stumbling about in the dark could drop a chap over a crag a hundred feet or more, and there was no water unless he was extremely lucky. Once located, word was sent to the nearest farmer or outback settler who eventually reached the missing man and restored him to civilisation and the SAAF transferred him back to base or hospital if needed. Three pupils were sent back to UK as a result of disobeying orders or injury after one of these adventures.

Night flying was another new and exciting experience, one I loved out there. I went solo after two hours' dual instruction. It was so refreshing flying around in the dark with only the tiny cockpit lights over the instruments to keep one company and looking out for the red and green navigating lights of other aircraft. The cool wind in one's face and the steady drone of the little Moth engine lulled one into a sense of security as she circled around the field. In the distance the bright lights of the towns and the city shone out like beacons, and the flickering goose-neck paraffin lamps of the flare-path were very reassuring. We all had some tricky moments trying to get down. Judgement of height between you and the ground when landing was dicy at first; you couldn't see the ground. The flare-path on each side was the only guide available. Three pupils were sent home, for the Chief Flying Instructor didn't think they were capable of flying solo at night and two smashed their undercarriage up after umpteen abortive attempts to get down. No one was severely injured but they were scrubbed off the course. Half-way through the course we had lost seven pupils, at the end the figure had risen to 10, one was killed in a forced landing in the desert, miles off course in the wrong direction in bushmen's territory.

My own progress continued according to schedule, and I thoroughly enjoyed every minute.

The course ended on 7 April. I passed the final flying test by the Chief Flying Instructor and academic, technical examinations by the Chief Ground Instructor were safely negotiated. When the results were posted on the notice board I was delighted to see I was assessed as a Group 1 pilot. The gods were still with me. I would go forward to an advanced school on single engined aircraft opening the door to be a fighter pilot. I had no desire to be a bomber pilot, the thought of chauffeuring a multi-engined aircraft straight and level gave me the horrors, all the fun of flying would be lost; not to mention the responsibility of the crew's lives in my hands. The bug of free flight had bitten me hard, I wanted to be my own master above everything else. I was absolutely ecstatic with joy and couldn't thank my instructors enough, my destiny lay in my own hands, I had to succeed. However, we all had a long way to go to gain our wings, a very sobering thought.

Some of us were posted to No 22 Air School, Vereeniging three days later. The airfield was still on the high plateau, and the training aircraft were to be our old friends of Grantham days – the twin-seater Harvards. These aircraft were more updated to Mark 2/3, more powerful than the first ever seen at Grantham. They had gained the reputation of a good service aircraft but hard to handle – it scared the daylights out of many pupils – but it was said that if one could fly the aircraft well, one could fly any single-seater operational aircraft that one was requiredto do. They had little vices that brought the best out of one, and were the last challenge before gaining the coveted 'wings' and becoming a fully fledged pilot.

It was now autumn in S.A., the weather slightly cooler, more cloudy, but still warmer than an English summer. Dress was much the same as at Potchefstroom. This air station was much more organised than our old school, it was a service flying training school, more disciplined and stricter in many ways, but nothing untoward if one was to make the grade. The instructors were the usual mixture of SAAF and RAF with equally high standards. A number of RAF instructors were resting between tours of operations, which didn't make them the easiest of instructors, they were inclined to be impatient and irascible in the early days. I drew Flying Officer 'Porky' as he was known.

He had problems getting in and out of the cockpit, which was the rear one in the case of these all metal monoplanes. The pupil sat in the front cockpit and all solo flying was done from the front one, entirely the opposite to the Tiger Moth. He had a terrible phobia of being killed by a pupil, to judge by his remarks – his temperament was completely different to Godkin's – impatient, highly strung, and expressively volatile.

We formed part of the 50 strong (B) Flight, another mixture of SAAF and RAF pupils from elementary flying training schools dotted around Jo'burg (the colloquial name for Johannesburg). For the first time the five occupants of our room were all RAF and a strong companionship was formed between us. We were all from different backgrounds but a wide gulf separated us intellectually, and socially.

Johnny Dick, my bosom pal for many months to come, was a rigger in the Clydeside shipyards, a well-built red-headed Scotsman with a large ginger moustache. Gordon, the son of an air commodore, was very timid and an introvert, fair-haired and slightly built with a stammer. He kept a parrot as a pet, which he had bought in Mombasa and clung to ever since: Johnny said in a frivolous moment that he only needed a wooden leg to complete the picture, but Gordon hadn't a sense of humour we soon learnt and was rather taciturn. Don was an undergrad surveyor, very handsome chap, sporting a small neat moustache and straight black hair; he had a quiet studious manner. Ruddy-faced Ken had a bearing more akin to a dumpy naturalist; he looked older than his years, and was in fact an architect. He had short mousy hair and his shorts seemed too long for his legs. His whole dress didn't seem to fit him properly; he seemed out of place, always wearing more clothing than was necessary, wearing thick underclothing underneath his shirt and a bush-shirt on top of that! His ungainly manner was not the personification of a fighter pilot or an officer, despite his degree.

Johnny and I felt a little out of place in the initial stages of moving in with these middle and upper class types, Johnny more so than I; he felt distinctly uncomfortable. He was basically a quiet chap for a Glaswegian and in this company he had an inferiority complex. This was understandable to a certain extent, but he didn't reach this stage without hard work and displaying as much dedication and acumen as his fellow room mates. I learnt later how wrong I was in my estimation of his character.

Being a regular serving airman with a great deal of experience of all types, they held no terrors for me. Some chaps that I held in high esteem in my earlier days of training had fallen by the wayside, and they were the most likeable chaps one could wish to meet. We all settled down to live together harmoniously. The only discordant note was from the bally parrot. It was obvious that Don, Gordon and Ken would undoubtedly be commissioned if they completed the course; whereas Johnny and I hoped the class-conscious hierarchy would lower their sights. We were all classed as cadets in South Africa whatever one's rank or role was before. Surprisingly the SAAF senior officers proved to be more class-conscious than the British – probably apartheid, army rank and training, a comparatively new force, and the fact that all aircrew were officers were the basic factors. It was hard to define. Strictly speaking they had a very small military air force before the war worthy of the name, they had no modern aircraft until the RAF shipped them there.

Nevertheless our little group knitted well together, we didn't have the same flying instructors but we attended lectures together. Most of the ground instructors were SAAF and most flying instructors were RAF. For the purpose of marching from one lecture room to another, a cadet Flight leader was appointed and two sub-section leaders, of which I was one. The leader wore his white lanyard and we wore red ones.

No 22 Air School was entirely different to Potchefstroom; this was a more proficient, highly organised service establishment as opposed to the relaxed flying club atmosphere of 6 Air School. Native army guards were everywhere here; khaki drill uniform, red fez, and carrying an assegai. The security was necessary at this airfield, Vereeniging was a political hotbed inhabited for the most part by the die-hard Afrikaners, and our first real encounter with the descendants of the old Boer faction.

Hostility made itself very apparent here; a SA Army camp was situated on the other side of the town and they wore the green flash on their shoulder straps which indicated they were home defence troops only. That was one way of putting it, the real truth was – they refused to leave the country to fight in support of the Allies and the constitution of the country permitted them to do so. They hated the British and resented our presence.

The South African Air Force had many fighter squadrons operating in the Middle East, usually flying Tomahawks and Kittyhawks and they took part in the successful operations in Italy, the Baltic States and Greece. Their hero was 'Sailor' Malan, who with his countrymen, joined the RAF; fought in the Battle of Britain and became a top scoring ace.

Flying training commenced on the Harvard, a vast difference to our old Tiger Moths; A much heavier metal monoplane, it was much more complicated with flaps, retractable undercarriages, two-pitch airscrews, instrument panel and a mass of gauges all calibrated to the American system, neither metric nor standard, and a whole host of extra controls that seemed insurmountable to master after the first trip. I liked the aircraft from the beginning, it stood higher off the ground for taxying; one sat in the front giving an unobstructed view ahead, a large clear canopy covering a large cockpit. No puny controls, instruments clear and everything conveniently placed. An adjustable seat and a radio, and the best thing of all, when the hood was closed, one sat in a windless shell with only a steady drone from the engine. No airstream whipping one's face and shoulders, no goggles required except for take-off and landing, when the hood was pushed back as a safety measure.

There was a great deal more cockpit-drill to carry out, before starting the engine, running it up to test the magnetos, taxying to the take-off point and the last check before turning into wind and taking-off. This all had to be memorized and applied as second nature, before the serious work of actually learning to fly the machine. The first weeks were hard work with no time for frivolities; we studied in every spare minute the layout of the cockpit and the functions of every knob, switch and control, memorizing engine and coolant temperatures, hydraulic gauge pressures etc. most of which was in the American idiom. Then we had to try to apply our new knowledge in practice. There were numerous incidents that upset nervous instructors, such as pupils with their hand on the wrong lever, trying to retract the undercarriage instead of the flaps – whilst still on the ground! Chaps who didn't know their left foot from the right, subsequently applying the wrong brake and colliding with bowsers or stationary aircraft; trying to take off in coarse pitch instead of fine: retracting the flaps in mistake for the undercarriage just after take-off and consequently dropping like a stone before climbing speed was attained. Most of these clangers (mistakes) were of course due to nerves and apprehension, not so much ability. Listening to an instructor haranguing the unfortunate pupil on the apron was hilarious, if one wasn't involved.

Instructors' vocabulary was the most extensive and expressive I've ever heard. I never had any of these problems, old Porky kept his hand firmly on the flap levers and held them like a vice, there was no way any action of a pupil was going to deposit him on mother earth during the take-off. He was a great chap, obscene observations flowed from him like a river in full flood. He once said to me. 'The bloody Germans tried to kill me, and I thought that was the end of it – but you are doing your bloody best to finish the job, you bloody idiot.'

For all that the little fat chap was a damned good instructor. I thoroughly enjoyed flying the Harvard, with its 600 hp radial engine aerobatics were easier; it was easier to land, being heavy and not inclined to float halfway down the airfield after cutting the engine; and of course it wasn't subjected to so many air currents, thus giving a smoother flight. Her maximum height was 21,000 ft and she could reach 210 mph at 5,000 ft, the normal height for exercises; a tremendous difference to the little Moth. They were all painted silver with black flashes which enhanced the impression that one was flying a solid operational aircraft. Indeed they were, they were equipped to carry machine-guns and bombs.

After a thorough work-out, spinning, stalling, climbing and descending turns, engine assisted landings and forced landings I was checked by Flying Officer Leete and made my first solo in the Harvard after 6.30 hours dual instruction. Porky was the first to congratulate me.

'Well done lad, if you kill me before the end of the course, I'll never forgive you.' He had a dry sense of humour, but he was also a cynic and he wasn't the type that could be patronised or taken advantage of. From now until the final progress test, was the last lap. I resolved that nothing would deter me from someone pinning those golden wings on my chest.

Once again, training was stepped up with more complicated exercises, the inevitable hairy recovery from spinning practised by oneself, engineless forced landings on strips and the usual aerobatics that one made a complete botch of at times, leaving one hanging by his straps upside down. This was the really dicy period, more chaps were scrubbed in this period than any other. No silly mistakes from now on would have any sympathetic hearing, one was to all intents and purposes a pilot and one was expected to behave like one and dedicate oneself to the perfection of one's trade. The smallest deviation or mistake was enough to say goodbye to a flying career. Major accidents happened to the most unlikely chaps, whilst flying solo, but one was supposed to be proficient enough to avoid them now. The top pupil, a South African, was court-martialled for doing a slow-roll over the airfield at 300 feet! This was a disciplinary offence, so he spent a long time in a Pretoria military prison. Others were grounded for landing with their undercarriage retracted; for bad airmanship, which meant that their flying was a danger to others; and unauthorised low-flying.

In a community such as ours a secret couldn't be kept very long. Clerks inadvertently disclosed information in the Flight hut, ears picked up confidential conversations quite by accident. Johnny and myself learnt we were up to standard, but our room mates were not doing too well. They were all below par in their individual flying performances and no doubt would be well aware of it. If they knew of our successful headway, they never mentioned it. Johnny and I were extremely happy, we couldn't subdue our feelings unfortunately and I rather think that the others knew why. Their superior academic qualities were away ahead of ours, there was no doubt of that, but if one's flying was not up to standard, that was of no account.

The course progressed, getting easier I thought, but old Porky in the back seat was constantly telling me to 'get my finger out', he hated my aerobatics, spinning and stalling, or so he vehemently said. If he didn't get a smooth operation he burnt my ears off, he particularly didn't like hanging by his straps. I once remarked in a flippant tone, 'Hang on to your bangers,' doing a roll off the top. For what seemed an eternity a deathly hush descended and then a gurgle was heard in my headphones – I thought he was having a choking fit – then a roar that required no headphones to hear what an incompetent, impudent, b. . . . . I was. 'I'll show you, you b. . . . . I've got her!' He then proceeded to try to tear the aircraft to bits in an exhibition of combat flying I had never witnessed before. The 'G' force was terrific, I blacked out three times, an entirely new experience. He threw her all over the sky and to be honest I thought we were never to come out of one dive – I think he was of the same mind – he frightened himself.

When we landed he looked at me and said, 'Are you ok?' I assured him I was, I apologized for my stupid remark and said it was the best flying I had ever experienced. He grinned through his pallid face; it had obviously taken a great deal out of him, and he said, 'You're a cheeky beggar, you'll go far lad, I haven't flown like that for years and I don't think I will repeat it.' He didn't elucidate on his connotation of how far I would go and in what direction! He got something out of his system; he might not have liked instructing, but in my opinion he under-estimated himself, I grew to like him more and more. Hidden behind that taciturn manner I believed we had a lot in common. If it wasn't for the network of spies, I would have had no knowledge of my progress; he never praised anyone. However nothing could be taken for granted, anything could happen before the end of the course; don't count your chickens before they hatched, was the axiom.

We had two one-hour sessions of dual night-flying without incident, and two days later I was down in the book for a solo test. The first two nights' exercises were taking off and landing on a flare path formed of goose-neck paraffin flares, instrument flying, and a cross-country navigational flight. The more formidable task of landing was assisted by a floodlight parked on the end of the grass runway. From starting up the engine, everything looked and sounded so different, surrounded by a new atmosphere of night-time and flaming exhausts. This, the third night, the duty book read 15-mins dual with Porky, then a solo check with another instructor and, if found proficient enough, I'd fly my first solo.

Porky arrived late in a hell of a flap; the air was blue – I guessed he must have over-indulged at dinner in the mess that night – and his car came to a screaming halt alongside our Harvard. I had already started up on orders from the airfield controller, and having completed the drill she was ticking over nicely when he arrived. The ground controller ordered us to take up position at the check-point near the mobile ground control trailer and, with old Porky struggling to get in the rear cockpit as usual, he banged on the fuselage and waved me away.

As I taxied to the trailer as fast as I dared, I heard a thud at the back of me, but pressed on regardless – it was Porky falling head first into the cockpit as I swung her rapidly round a stationary aircraft. I didn't know it then, of course. I had barely time to do the last check-list before take-off when the green lamp flashed urgently, giving me permission to enter the flare-path and take off. The intercom was dead.

Half-flap, pitch fine, mixture rich, ruddering in a straight line, I gave her the gun and off we went, levelling out, and with a slight backward pressure of the stick she took off like a bird. Up undercarriage, climb to 300 feet watching air speed rise to 115 mph to stop her dropping like a stone – when flaps were raised – then trim elevator to climb and away we went. I was concentrating on the instrument panel, the ASI (air speed indicator) and the altimeter to do a climbing turn to the left when there was a click in the headphones and a gurgle that sounded like a drowning man!

A distant voice came through the headphones. 'Whatever you do, don't panic.' I was nonplussed. I had never heard Porky use that expression before. Then came a great roar, 'Some bloody idiot has taken the stick out of the rear cockpit and not replaced it. I have no control whatever, damn it; do you hear Ashman – I've got no bloody control.' A pause for breath, while I'm on the down-wind leg. 'My bloody life is in your hands, do you understand!' Well, I was astounded by this one-in-a-million turn of events, so instead of turning to land I went round again whilst I composed myself. The situation didn't frighten me – I was quite confident. I never said a word.

The intercom clicked on again and a much more controlled, quieter voice said, 'Look laddy, you are going to land this kite, just keep your finger out, don't panic and you will put her down in one piece. You know the bloody drill, just follow it and I'll buy you a pint.' My vocal cords had dried up, but I said, 'OK sir, I've a stake in this too. I have no desire to pack it in either.' I heard a slight gurgling and the intercom went silent. I flew her back to the down-wind leg and went through the normal drill of lowering undercarriage, lowering flaps, selecting fine pitch, and adjusted the trim and throttling back to 95 mph.

Turning into the wind and aligning the aircraft with the flare-path, I realised we were a little short of it. I was about to open the throttle for an engine-assisted approach when a voice bawled in my ear, 'You are not going to make it. Go round again.' I replied in as calm a voice as my vocal cords would allow, 'I am in control, sir, let me get on with it!' A deathly hush descended on us. A few more revs with the throttle brought the nose up with slight back pressure on the stick, and she skated over the boundary in a shallow approach, slightly nose-up, elevators trimmed; then she sank like a feather, the wheels touching and rolling along without a bump. Throttle cut, the tail dropped and with the stick hard back into my stomach – we were down.

Nothing was said until we reached the holding point on the airfield and switched off. I climbed out and waited until he extracted himself and his parachute from his cockpit. Expecting the worst, I felt really miserable, the engine-assisted landing was one of the best I had ever done, even in daylight; but my impertinence was another thing. He walked up to me, looked me full in the face in the dim light of a flare and said, 'Bloody good show, boy; I should have checked that everything was in order before we took off. It was entirely my fault, and when I find out who took the stick away I'll have his guts for garters.' Praise indeed, and coming from him it was akin to being knighted by the King. As he moved off he turned and remarked, 'I thought I'd had my chips.' I was booked for another flight that night but he felt unwell and left. Lieutenant Alexander, Flight Commander, approached me and said, 'Get in, I'm giving you a solo test.' With a laugh, I said, 'You will have to find the missing stick first'. 'If you are having me on, boy, I'll stick it up your backside,' he barked. When I explained, he was horrified.

The control columns were normally in place in both cockpits; the only time the rear one was removed was when a pilot flew solo, to prevent it fouling anything that may come lose in the cockpit. It was fixed in a clip out of the way and the harness was also fastened to prevent it flying about. Someone had removed the rear column for a pupil going solo, but they hadn't put it in the clip where it could be recovered and slotted in the orifice at the bottom of the cockpit control rod. Porky had been so busy strapping himself in that he didn't notice the clip was empty until we were on our way! Lieutenant Alexander SAAF took one from another aircraft and away we went on test with no trouble. Unfortunately, the aircraft developed an engine fault and he couldn't send me solo that night. Strictly speaking, I had already gone solo with Porky as a passenger, but it didn't count; and it was prudent not to have the temerity to mention it, under the circumstances.

The course neared its last stage and life speeded up becoming much more varied and exacting, Squadron Leader Kennedy passed me for further training on to the last stage of the course. The stiffest test I had so far flown. Porky was no longer my sole instructor from April onwards. Most of them were SAAF instructors, six in all but seldom consecutively. I was extremely sorry about this state of affairs. I missed Porky funnily enough, we had a rapport between us that I never realised before. The new brigade specialised in various aspects of flying: pilot navigation, instrument flying, dive bombing, air to air gunnery, air to ground gunnery, formation flying, low flying, night flying across country, landing and taking off in formation, and so on. They were individuals that one never got close to; one was expected to be a competent pilot by now and they concentrated solely on the exercises they were there to teach us. Once taught it was left to the pupil to practise them solo until one achieved perfection. It was without doubt the most exciting, adventurous part of the course, one day one was dive bombing a target and the next shooting at a drogue or a ground target, or going on a long cross-country navigational flight to more odd sounding airfields viz Kromdraadrift, Jackalskraal, Keukermuir, Edenville, Rysmierbuilt, Lynkloof etc with only a map and a compass.

One day old Porky turned up to keep a look out whilst I did some instrument flying under the hood. He seemed a different person, pleased to see me and told me he kept a fatherly eye on my progress.

My mates were also preoccupied with the last stages, little time for anything but study. Johnny worked the hardest in ground subjects but he seemed to be content with his flying. Ken and Gordon would pass their ground examinations easily, Don would too I thought, but Johnny and I would have a hard task ahead of us. It all depended on the paper we were given in each subject, Johnny was clever with practical tests such as armaments. The Browning machine gun was the very devil to assemble, gunnery and aero engines were his forte. A pilot was expected to service his own aircraft and re-arm it in the event of an emergency. I was well up on the theory of flight, theory of gunnery and bombing, aerodynamics, and meteorology; so we helped each other as much as possible. For the last month of the course, I flew solo on every flight, flying instruction was completed – it only remained for me to practise and improve my standard before the final test.

I thoroughly enjoyed dive-bombing, not so much for the bombing, but because it was invaluable for learning how to position the aircraft for a wing over to dive on to the target in a straight line. Having done it solo I wasn't greatly interested in the results and it was of no account. I hit the target a few times but bombing wasn't my scene. Gunnery was.

At the beginning of August we commenced sitting our final ground exams both orally and written, and the worst part for me was the interviews with a specially convened board. Probing psychological questions: did I want to be an instructor? Did I want to fly fighters or bombers? What kind of aircraft, did I enjoy flying? Did I enjoy the training? Had I any complaints to make about the training or the instructors etc? It was carefully planned to find any weakness in one's character.

On 14 August I presented myself to Captain Upton for the final flying test. He was extremely pleasant and reassuring, I was a nervous wreck. This was it, the ultimate test, one either passed or not, there were no second chances. The aircraft responded beautifully to the controls and for 50 minutes – believe me it seemed an eternity – she was asked to perform every manoeuvre in the book; 50 minutes in air time is a long time when in action *all* the time, and not just sitting there as a passenger.

Captain Upton sat quietly, giving orders, making no remarks whatever. Nothing could be deduced from his demeanour of what he thought about the execution of the orders he gave. When we landed he climbed out of the cockpit, noted my name again and said crisply, 'OK, you have passed.'

'Thank you, sir,' I said. He just grinned and said with a debonair wave of his hand, 'Don't thank me, boy. It's my pleasure.'

A little fat figure came rushing out of the flight office after having a word with the captain on his way in. It was Porky. He had cut a flight short – when he saw the entry in the book of my final test – to be down on my return, leaving his pupil sitting in the aircraft. He was overjoyed, beaming all over his face he shook hands and congratulated me, banging me on the back saying he knew I would do it.

Gradually over a couple of days my friends came into our room all smiles and we knew they had passed; it was congratulations all round. Johnny was the last, we all fidgeted restlessly looking out of our room waiting for him to appear at the end of the path leading to the billet until he appeared when we all rushed out to meet him, trying to read his face. Typically, Johnny remained impassive until he couldn't hold it any longer and his face split, with that large moustache, into a huge grin and we knew all was well. He had revealed himself as a mercurial character as time went by, and he and I were inseparable.

We avidly watched the flight notice board for our assessments, when they were published they caused considerable surprise to everyone. More so to me than most. Out of the whole flight of 50, nine failed at various stages or in the finals. Of the 41 successful pupils, 32 received a commission with the rank of pilot officers, the remainder of which I was one, were promoted to sergeant pilots. The examination results were an eye-opener; I was third top in flying and eighth in ground subjects. Johnny was fifth in flying and fifteenth in ground subjects. Don, Ken and Gordon were all in the first ten in ground subjects but in the mid and lower twenties for flying. Don, Ken and Gordon received their commissions; Johnny and I were sergeants. The system was enigmatic to say the least, to Johnny and me it was ludicrous. We suspected the outcome from the very beginning of course as the reader will remember, but no one expected the system to be so illogical and autocratic after the results of the examinations were published. It proved the old school-tie system was unbeatable. We were disgusted but put a brave face on it.

Some SAAF pupils from Germiston were to be presented with their wings in conjunction with our flight of (B) Squadron simultaneously, making up a passing out parade of roughly 60 pilots. All our friends were invited as guests to attend, so we were kept busy writing invitations to our hosts who had made our stay in South Africa as enjoyable as they could. John and I had hundreds, it was a blessing in a way that they couldn't all attend, the airfield was taken over by thousands of guests that couldn't be catered for. The great day dawned with bags of spit and polish and everyone in high spirits. The parade went off without a hitch in the usual manner. The ceremony was honoured by the Prime Minister, Field Marshal Jan Smuts. He pinned the Wings brevet on our tunics as our names were called and he wished us luck in our next stage. We all felt like heroes, extremely happy.

All acrimony put aside, the terrible twins, as Johnny and I were known, organised a private celebration in the mess for the whole flight and their instructors that night. We had a whip round and coerced the stewards by bribery – they were the poor Kaffirs or Bantus who waited on at meal times – to lay it all on. The biggest contributors were the SAAF ex-pupils, who were exceedingly generous. The instructors poured in and I was quite overcome when old Porky turned up, I was master of ceremonies and greeted all the instructors. The sight of him beaming all over his face in his best uniform striding through the foyer made my day.

We had a smashing party, Porky chatted with us all night and I discovered that he had a sense of humour for the first time and furthermore he was an acrobat, the way he did somersaults over the settees was astonishing. After months of watching him struggling to get in that rear cockpit it was unbelievable; surprising what a bottle of gin could do. How he must have ached the next day. A rough time lay ahead for his pupils in the morning.

I discovered that he had been a Hurricane pilot in the Middle East and took part in operation 'Torch', he was shot down defending convoys for Malta, landing in the drink. Those of us who knew the background to the ME appreciated the fast and furious action he must have gone through. The Battle of Britain had always hogged the headlines but the public was never made aware of the more fierce fighting under much more adverse conditions in North Africa and over Malta. He was hospitalised for some time and unfortunately he put on weight through glandular trouble, so he was taken off operations and after an instructors' course, sent to the Union. My assessment for instrument flying was 'above average' and I had him to thank for that in particular, and my immense success in general flying.

My mind was set on day-fighters and he was the man that made it all possible, I was indeed indebted to him, although he told me later – and I say this in all modesty – I was a natural pilot.

I had taken the first hurdle in my stride, my future looked settled and I was eager to get away to start the next course. I hoped I wasn't going to miss the end of the war, not from any sense of bravado on my part, I had this intrinsic feeling that it was still incumbent upon me to prove I really had what it takes – as the Americans would say.

*

A mixed party of ex-pupils including Johnny and myself was formed to travel north and we left on 7 October 1944 for Egypt aboard a SAAF Lodestar. We went via Ndola (Northern Rhodesia), Nairobi (Kenya) to Entebbe (Uganda) on the northern shore of the vast Lake Victoria for an overnight stop. Thence to Khartoum (Sudan) and the last lap to Cairo by Dakota.

Our contingent was sent to an Aircrew Reception Centre at Heliopolis a few miles away from Cairo to await further posting. It wasn't until we arrived that I realised our original 'B' Flight from Vereeniging had shrunk. The Lodestar that brought us up from the south was limited to about 30 passengers and Ken and Gordon were not amongst them. What their fate was, we would never know. We were reduced now to three of the five room-mates who had been together for eight months – Don, Johnny and myself. We had a week to explore Cairo; Don was now in the officers' mess so we didn't see much of him. Johnny and myself befriended another sergeant pilot, Sandy Mitchell. He got his wings at Kroonstad; he was a smashing chap; full of fun but with a placid, altruistic nature. We had a wonderful time touring the city and taking in the usual sights such as the Pyramids, Museums, etc.

Our postings came through, Don was to go to an OTU (Operational Training Unit) at Fayid, an airfield south of Suez, to train on the American fighter 'Thunderbolt'. This was bad news. We all knew that these very heavy fighters were now in action in the Far East, so on completion of the course he would be Burma-bound, not what he hoped for and not a pleasant prospect. Although we had all been trained to survive in the jungle (if one lived after being shot down), none of us ever thought that we would have need for it, so it wasn't taken seriously. It came as a shock. With some trepidation we sergeants awaited our fate with fingers crossed, the Thunderbolts were the most insensitive aircraft anyone could fly. But the gods were with us once again, Johnny, Mitch and myself were posted to 71 OTU, Ismailia where we knew they operated Hurricanes and Spitfires. At last my dream was coming true or the chance was being given to me to fulfil it. Phlegmatic Johnny was excited as I was, he wasn't ambitious and I always felt that he didn't give himself enough credit. He was so reticent when previous discussions had turned to our future prospects, he gave the impression that he couldn't throw off his inferiority complex. Yet the same man off duty was mercurial, the life and soul of the party.

Next day Don left from the officers' mess for Fayid, and we three departed for Ismailia on the west bank of the Suez Canal. The two stations were 60 miles apart and it was impossible to make contact. Later I had a letter telling me he was posted to India, but heard no more. Our contingent arrived at 71 OTU, Ismailia on 10 October to form Course No 69. Johnny and myself were the only two representatives from 22 Air School, Vereeniging.

IV

A Fighter Pilot is Born

Ismailia was half-way down the Suez Canal, 50 miles from Port Said and north of the Bitter Lakes which formed part of it. The town was just a collection of clap-board and native style breeze-block buildings with absolutely nothing to recommend it, except a first-class metal road leading to the one and only lifting road bridge across the canal to Palestine (Israel) and points east, built by the British. The town had no attractions whatsoever for Europeans, especially for us.

It seemed many years ago since I first saw the canal en route for South Africa. I was so excited then, with the wonder of it all; the first sight of an ancient world was exhilarating to an unsophisticated chap such as myself. Living on the land in tents also gave me an affinity with the country and the atmosphere made a deep impression on me. Now, however, I was a year older in age but much more sophisticated. It had been a very long year, the longest in my life. If the country hadn't changed, I had. The civilised RAF station washed away the old sentiments and we were to see little of what I remembered of our happy-go-lucky days in the desert. The camps had gone and nature had reasserted itself.

The weather was different now, becoming much cooler as winter approached. It wasn't noticeable during the day, but very much so when the sun went down. The sudden change of temperatures from day to night was severe.

The aerodrome was a typical peacetime RAF station, an empire base of numerous operational squadrons of the past. Modernised brick buildings, our permanent quarters were clean, hygienic, two-storey custom-built, with showers and all mod-coms. The pilots' mess was segregated from the station sergeants' mess, but quite comfortable and adequate; we had no fees to pay either, and that brought huge smiles to our faces. The first object of interest was the layout of two intersecting concrete runways, the first we had ever seen. Grass fields gave more scope for take-off and landing. We were thrilled to look around the Hurricanes and Spitfires standing in neat rows along the strips of metalled parking bays in a regimental straight line, and hear for the first time the unmistakable throaty roar of a Merlin engine. They all looked and sounded like thoroughbreds. During my service in England I hadn't seen many modern fighters; the Battle of Britain had passed me by. But I was completely *au fait* with the exploits of the Hurricane, the aircraft that took the brunt of the fighting in the very early days of my service. So it was with some pride and sentiment I looked on these old fighters, now relegated to training and introducing new pilots to the intricacy of flying single-seaters.

Johnny, Mitch and I kept together in the same room and after sorting ourselves out domestically, we lay on our beds in deep thought. Gradually we all began expressing our fears and doubts. After looking in the cockpits of the aircraft and seeing the vast array of instruments and controls which were entirely different to the Harvard led to our first misgiving. The next one was the inescapable fact that the first time we flew any one of them, we would be on our own with no instructor sitting there to pull us out of trouble. There were no dual-seater fighters of course. It was a big step for raw pilots to step into an entirely strange aircraft. A strong bond was formed between the three of us. We had different natures but there was an indefinable link which was unbreakable. Mitch came from nowhere and fitted into Johnny's and my lives like a jigsaw. We never had an argument or a wrong word to say about each other, and would defend any one of us to the death. We became known as the 'Three Musketeers' amongst the rest of the course, and endeavoured to fly with each other when it was feasible.

No 69 Course consisted of 30 pilots, a mixture of fledglings such as our trio, some ex-operational pilots who were retraining from other types such as the Kittyhawk, Tomahawks etc, and others who hadn't flown operationally – instructors, drogue-pilots, etc who had volunteered for a change and reassessed for operational flying. Johnny and myself were the only two from the original crowd who gained their wings at Vereeniging. The rest had gone to other OTUs on different aircraft, or sent home as non–operational pilots.

This was a feather in our caps; to my knowledge every one of the chaps who flew with us at Vereeniging wanted to fly the Spitfire. This cheered us up when things weren't going too well. We worried needlessly the first night, for the next day cleared up some doubts. We hadn't noticed the few Harvards on our arrival, but we learned that we would be checked thoroughly in these aircraft before going on to Hurricanes in the normal course of events. We would not have reached this far of course if there had been any doubts about our capabilities, but it was nice to know that we were not to be thrown in the deep end immediately.

The instructors here were a hard core of battle-proven pilots, but they were a great bunch of chaps. They treated us as equals and respected us as pilots and not as pupils, so a warm rapport was built up between us. Pilot Officer Hall, a young chap and the only one not to have seen any active service put me through my paces on the Harvard. Three trips of one hour each to cover everything in the book. Satisfied, he passed me on to the Hurricane section.

Ground work during this time was fully occupied by studying the layout of the Hurricane's cockpit, memorizing all the pilot's handling notes, etc. After three days we were examined on our knowledge of the recommended temperatures, pressures, speeds and the whereabouts of the controls blindfolded. We had spent hours sitting in the cockpit and going through the drill without even starting the engine, which wasn't allowed. On 1 November after flying a Harvard solo, the instructor told me my moment of truth had come, and climbed into Hawker Hurricane Mark IId HV591 for my first flight.

I gave the signal to the ground crew to start, after going through the pre-starting check, and she roared into life. What a sound! Surrounded by ground crew and instructors I went through the various checks to make sure that all the needles were pointing to the correct position on the dials, running it up with two chaps lying on the tail plane and checking the magnetos, I was ready to taxi out. With a wave of the hand the chocks were removed from the wheels and away I went, jockeying along the narrow perimeter track to the head of the runway in use. It was quite a moment, in charge of a fully operational aircraft that took the brunt of the Battle of Britain; apart from the fact that I had never flown it before and had no knowledge of what to expect from the moment of take-off, this was a test of character as opposed to ability. I had to prove to everyone, including myself, that all my instructors' confidence in me from Sywell onwards, was not misplaced.

Probably thousands of chaps had felt the same way before me, but at that moment it was very personal. I was going to succeed or die in the attempt. It sounds very melodramatic but when one didn't know how a strange aircraft was going to behave, it was an inescapable fact. Receiving permission to taxi onto the runway and take off, I went through the drill and away we went with no trouble at all. After one circuit of the airfield she landed without the slightest tendency to bounce on that very wide, solid undercarriage. At the flight hut I received the usual accolades from everyone, I had flown my first operational aircraft and for the first time I felt I was entitled to the wings on my chest.

In alphabetical order – which frequently happened – I was the first of our trio to go, but Johnny and Mitch accomplished it with little fuss, much to our relief and happiness. This was only the beginning of an intensive course. We were trained in battle formation and fighter tactical manoeuvres on the Harvards with our instructors and then repeated it solo. The same exercises in the Hurricanes followed, plus instrument flying in cloud. Close formation, aerobatics, forced landings, spinning, stalling, and D/F (direction finding) navigation kept us busily employed without much time off for leisure.

I found aerobatics in the Hurricane harder work than in the Harvard. Its main redeeming features were that it had a much tighter turn, making it possible to blackout, whereas the Harvard would stall and go into a spin before sufficient 'G' force was applied and that the Hurricane was much easier to land. It had a much more powerful engine of course in the Rolls-Royce 1,280 hp engine and its maximum speed was over 300 mph at 22,000 ft and considerably faster at lower heights.

It was difficult to believe that these aircraft were the main front line fighters in the Battle of Britain, outnumbering Spitfires; but their sterling performances as we all know, were sufficient to hold the Luftwaffe at bay at the most crucial time in our history and their exploits at Malta over the Med could not be surpassed. It was much faster than the Harvard of course and one could grow to love its rather clumsy handling. It had a high performance in the right hands, of that there was no doubt. It was an easy plane to fly with no vices, when one got used to handling it roughly and making corrections for every movement of the control column, slightly counter-acting them, rather like a car that oversteers on corners. The cockpit had limited viewing all round due to the small perspex panels in the hood. The frames of these panels were a darned nuisance and could have been responsible for the deaths of many pilots in combat.

However I considered it an honour to be given the opportunity to fly this historic aircraft.

Formation flying took priority. On these runways it was possible to take off in a 'V' formation of five aircraft, and remain in the same tight formation in every manoeuvre when airborne. Both on the runway and in the air we found it hard work to keep station of one wing length away from the Hurricane one was formating on. After that, 'battle' formations of sections of four, six, and eight aircraft, which would be the formations used in actual operations, were the order of the day until we could take station without a second thought. Our trio enjoyed every minute of it. It felt wonderful to be in charge of one's own fighter and the only instructor was the leader of the formation, who had eyes in the back of his head, or so it seemed, when he gave someone a rousting over the radio to keep up and not to stray or kindly keep out of his lap.

We discovered an Arab encampment lay behind our sleeping quarters, on the opposite side of the 'Sweet Water Canal'. The canal was a huge joke to us but not so funny when we learnt of its reputation! It wasn't so much a canal that led into the Suez Canal, as a shallow, wide, irrigation ditch which stank to high heaven. Along the bank on our side was a high barbed-wire fence, to keep the occupants of the encampment out and prevent RAF personnel falling in. From our window we could observe the daily routine of the encampment which consisted of mud huts with straw-covered roofs. Whether these people were displaced persons we never knew. The women were dressed in black robes with their faces covered, but the men only wore loin-cloths, more akin to Indians than Arabs, who were generally clothed from head to foot, only the face showing, hundreds of children and goats abounded everywhere. The men and children bathed in the foul water after squatting on the bank to relieve themselves! It was a ghastly sight only to be superseded, when the women carrying huge water urns on their heads, waded into it to fill them up from the same spot. The water was static making the situation more horrible. These people drank it, bathed, used it as toilet, and scrubbed their clothes in this foul, stinking, stagnant canal – it was incredible. If the breeze was in the wrong direction we had to keep the windows tightly closed, for there was no air-conditioning.

The station medical officer told us that some stupid erks, well under the influence, had fallen into the canal from a bridge which spanned it outside the station boundary. They had gone to town and drunk some illicit hooch. On the way back they acted the goat on some girders and lost their balance. Although they were inoculated, as we all were, against every known tropical disease, one died and the rest of the party were seriously ill for a very long time. The diseases didn't affect the Arabs because they were born with the inherent anti-bodies. Needless to say, we had already kept our distance from this cesspool after our previous observations. That weekend we had a break, taking the train to Cairo and on to Alexandria. There was little to be seen there, so we returned to Cairo and spent a tranquil time sailing on the Nile in the traditional feluccas – this design of one-sail boat went back centuries, to the days of the Pharaohs. We slept at a Services Club. Regretfully we were unable to reach Luxor due to lack of transport.

On our return we learned that our days on the Hurris were finished and we were transferred to the Spitfire section. We had constantly studied the layout and the controls of the Spit since our arrival; they were different again to the Hurri and the cockpit was tiny compared with the Hurri and Harvard. The whole aircraft was diminutive, standing on spindly legs that looked too close together compared with the Hurricane, but her beautiful lines were a picture. No aircraft in the world equalled her aesthetically in anyone's eyes. The one jarring obtrusion on this Mark V was the very large tropical air intake under the nose, essential, and fitted to all Mark V Spitfires in the Middle East. This was a modification to dissipate the excessive engine heat in hot climes – to put it simply, and not bore the reader with technical details. There were no preparations this time for our first solo.

Twelve days since my first flight in the Hurri, after 11 hours' flying time on it, my name was down in the flight book to fly my first Spitfire.

Every single one of these new experiences was a traumatic hurdle, exciting, adventurous, and laced with anxiety. This one was to top them all, or so I thought.

On the significant date of 13 November, under the watchful eye of Squadron Leader Ashton, gunnery officer, I took off in Spitfire No JK 984 on my first flight. The long nose was disturbing whilst taxying for it was impossible to see ahead and one was forced to taxi in a zigzag line to see where one was going. It was essential not to hang about; one had to make quick time to the runway before the engine overheated in the conditions prevailing, despite the overlarge radiator. Any pilot who had to switch off his engine before getting airborne owing to dangerous temperatures registered in the oil and coolant gauges, was on the mat. Dropping clangers (careless mistakes) like this upset the whole schedule, for the aircraft had to be towed back to the pad and allowed to cool off and them examined for further serviceability. Similarly, taking off meant getting the tail up as quickly as possible to steer a straight line down the runway, with the correct amount of rudder trim. The more powerful engine and lighter weight of the Spitfire, compared to the Hurricane and Harvard was a new experience and a joy when I became accustomed to it, but on the first trip it came as a surprise. She took off like a bird. I made little contribution to it, as she climbed away with gentle pressure backwards on the 'stick.' The only problem was the situation of the undercarriage lever.

Once trimmed for climbing at the correct boost and propeller pitch control she zoomed upwards with no effort. The controls were extrmely light to handle and seemed to know what one's next manoeuvre was going to be. It was like riding a bike, the slightest movement of the right hand on the control column was instantly obeyed. One of my attributes, or so I was told, was a sensitive touch, which was a disadvantage on the Harvard and on the Hurricane which both needed rougher treatment. Porky used to take me to task many times for not showing the aircraft who was the boss and forcing it to respond to my actions. The rougher one flew, according to him, the longer one would live in battle. It was an impossible situation at times, trying to please everyone.

This aircraft, however, was the supreme flying machine. The Spitfire was made to measure for me, sensitive in every way. We had an affinity from the very beginning. If anything she was too sensitive and did not like coarse or ham-fisted treatment. She was a lady, dainty and beautiful, albeit a very lethal one as I was to learn later. Why, I asked myself a thousand times over, had this come to me to me so late in the day? If it had only been a year earlier, or it hadn't taken so long frittering away time on immaterial training at ground schools, I could have doubled my flying time and into the thick of things from D-Day. This aircraft was the quintessence of all I had envisaged since I was thrown in the deep end at Sywell that summer day in August 1943, which was to change my whole life.

Aerobatics were a joy to perform in this aeroplane. With the high wing loading she required a higher speed in tight turns than the Hurricane and would flip out of one into a spin without warning, but one soon got used to treating her with respect, so little effort was needed. The trickiest manoeuvre was landing for she stalled at a higher speed than any other aircraft. Consequently the approach and landing speeds were higher, coupled with the blind approach due to the long nose and the tendency to float just above stalling speed at 90 mph down the runway before touch down. Landing without a bump on three points – the undercarriage wheels were only six feet apart – keeping her straight with the rudder on the runway with no direct forward vision brought the best out of pilots. Nevertheless I had the feeling I could put complete trust in her and she would not let me down. My faith was fully justified. If it was possible to have a love affair with an aircraft, this was it. She could be fickle, she could be temperamental, but handled with sympathy and firmness she was a dream. One had to have a feeling for the aeroplane to get the best out of her, just as a sensitive, soft-mouthed, highly-strung racehorse gives its all for a sympathetic rider.

With the Spitfire we were in a different division and training was more intensive. All previous exercises and manoeuvres on the Harvards and Hurricanes were repeated with the addition of low-flying, air to air and air to ground gunnery and new battle formation flying in a the latest guise of 'finger four' configuration of sections of four, eight and twelve. Low flying was what I liked best; there were miles of empty ground to practise over, nothing but desert and scrubland. Flying as low as 100 feet, one only then realised how fast a ground speed of 350 mph was. The sandy hillocks flashed by in a blur, and tremendous concentration was needed to bank and weave round the hillocks without flying into one. These exercises were all done on the east side of the Canal where we came across caravans threading their way through the dunes. Naturally, we could not avoid them at that height and speed, we were upon them before we knew it. They took a very dim view of it; it scared the trains of camels to death and caused tremendous confusion. Wandering tribes with their goats and camels were also encountered. Rifle shots were loosed off at us by the angry Arabs to no effect. It was the first time I had ever been shot at since some exciting nights with patrols at Grantham. We were encouraged by the instructors to beat up these people as good practice; it was necessary, as proven later. Nevertheless it was a dicy business; we learnt that some unfortunate

pilots who force-landed in this territory were never recovered dead
or alive and little of the aircraft was found by the Army's rescue
patrols in their armoured-cars. It was a sobering thought. It was
during one of these exercises, but this time in formation with seven
other Spitfires, I had a very narrow escape from cashing in my chips.

We were flying over the desert in formation at 300 feet when the
chap I was formating on became obscure. I thought a mist had arisen
from nowhere as it got thicker and thicker until I could barely see his
wing-tip, not ten yards away. Surely it couldn't be mist, not here
under the sun? It must be a sandstorm, yet there was no exceptional
turbulence which would have buffeted the aircraft about more than
usual over hot sand. I thought the instructor leading the section
would climb above it; this was ridiculous.

Concentrating on formating I didn't dare look ahead or around
me in case I collided with the next aircraft. After ten minutes or so I
realised that I couldn't see the instruments in the cockpit! It dawned
on me that the mist was inside the canopy. I was sitting in a steam
bath! Opening the canopy cleared it and looking at the gauges I saw
the coolant temperature was over boiling point, the engine oil
pressure gauge was in the red and the heat in the cockpit was
overpowering. Calling up the leader on the radio, I was told to return
to base immediately.

As I climbed to 2,000 feet turning towards base, the engine got
rougher and rougher, and an acrid oil-burning smell pervaded, even
with the canopy open. I knew instinctively that the engine would
seize up or blow up, but nothing in the world would induce me to
bale out before reaching civilisation in the Canal area. I nursed her
along for ten minutes, an eternity, until the Canal came in sight.
With speed dropping off and losing height, it was a battle to reach the
airfield.

Spot-on navigation brought the airfield directly ahead. This was
my last chance of baling out. At 500 feet it couldn't be left any later.
The cockpit was awash with coolant (Glycol), the heat unbearable,
and the black smoke belching out of the exhausts getting thicker by
the minute. I decided to land her but it was impossible to reach the
runway in use on the far side of the airfield. The engine bearings had
gone and clouds of smoke obscured my vision, so I switched off.
Heading for the nearest runway which happened to be across-wind –
not the runway in use – with a dead engine, and down to 100 feet I
had to do a tight turn and side-slip on the edge of the runway just

above stalling speed. With flaps and undercarriage down, she turned and sat down on all three points beautifully in one movement, a manoeuvre I had never had cause to practise before, but one out of the book, as they say. Keeping her straight down the runway with the coolant making a trail behind me as it ran out of the cockpit, I wasn't out of the wood yet. A Spitfire was taking off on the runway in use! A collision was avoided by a hair's-breadth at the intersection of the two runways by sheer luck, after I swerved the aircraft across and behind what I judged to be his take-off point. When she came to a halt I climbed out of the stinking cockpit, absolutely dazed, and thoroughly shaken. Two hairy consecutive incidents were shattering to say the least.

In no time at all, jeeps came screaming out from the control tower laden with officials and their retinue. I was expecting a pat on the back for getting down in the most exceptional circumstances for a sprog pilot – in one piece. It was exceedingly rare for a pupil to be put under such pressure due to any mechanical failure of an aircraft and of such proportions. Most accidents were due to pilot error. I was astounded when the airfield controller shouted:

'What the hell do you think you are playing at? Don't you realise you landed on the wrong bloody runway? You could have killed someone, you bloody fool!'

Well, that was more than I could take, I told him with all the invective I could muster, that if he was not fully aware of the circumstances he wasn't fit for his job, and he should apply for his pension post-haste before it was too late. I was exceedingly angry and didn't care a damn about the consequences of insubordination. I demanded he looked at the bloody engine, and then reiterate what he had just said.

'Don't you dare talk to me in that tone of voice,' he replied. 'You are a conceited ass, sergeant.'

At that moment another jeep arrived and I recognized the Chief Flying Instructor, Squadron Leader Ashton, who overheard the last few words. He told this controller to cut the cackle and tell him what the trouble was.

It was the very first time I'd lost my temper with an officer. The aircraft stood there enveloped in a blanket of heat haze that wasn't due to the sun. The cowlings were black, but he was so stupid he had not noticed it. Two senior officers in the party turned away and the airmen in the party grinned all over their faces at this debâcle, one I was deriving no pleasure from at all. An NCO fitter had a word in this flight lieutenant's ear after a cursory look at the aircraft; he couldn't touch the cowlings with his screwdriver to get them off, without burning his hands. The officers had a conflab out of hearing and looked abashed. The flight lieutenant tried to cover up his unwarranted tirade, much to the amusement of the ground crew, by issuing orders to them. With a peremptory, curt summons to get in the jeep, I was whisked off to the medical centre for the mandatory check-up, leaving the Spit to be towed in. The wheels of an investigation were immediately set in motion, I had to write my report and then give it orally to the CO of the station to verify it. The aircraft was examined by the engineering officer. He found that the coolant pump had been fitted wrongly, causing a leakage. The fitter responsible was disciplined as a consequence. I still felt bitter. I was no fool and I considered that I had nothing to prove to the controlling body and made no bones about it. Perhaps my idolatry of operational types was somewhat dented when they were of the rank of flight lieutenant and above. I may be candid but never conceited.

Before this stage I was a happy individual. Everything was going my way and I felt I owed the RAF a great deal, forgetting about my early years and traumatic situations I found myself in as an erk. The hair-raising experience I had just undergone was not easily forgotten, but could be overcome. What I could not stomach was the unprofessional attitude of the air traffic controlling officers. If they had been alert they would have heard the formation leader's orders and my distress call, alerted the emergency services to be on hand, and refused permission for the other chap to take off. Characteristically I investigated the circumstances prevailing in the control tower at the time, and I discovered that the officers had their faces in mugs of tea enjoying a cigarette and it was an airman on the staff who drew their attention to my landing. They saw nothing. It was they who had put the other pilot's life in jeopardy. No unjust criticism was going on my records without a fight, believe me, and I put that in my report.

In an interview with the CFI, he told me to try to erase the matter from my mind to recover my equilibrium and he took me up in a Harvard to restore confidence. Later on, I was summoned to HQ again, this time it was the station commander who wanted a word with me. He said he was looking into the matter but he was taking this opportunity to congratulate me, rather pompously I thought, 'on a very, courageous, tenacious piece of flying; up to the finest standards of the Royal Air Force.' He went on to say, 'You have saved a valuable aircraft, sergeant, and I will recommend you to higher authority for a commendation.' Taking it all with a pinch of salt, I thanked him respectfully, but told him I would be happy if I could resume flying immediately to which he readily agreed. I had been grounded whilst the incident was investigated, consequently losing a day's flying time and upsetting my schedule.

I always thought I was a congenial, phlegmatic person with a great deal of respect for aircrew, whatever category, albeit not so for administrative types unless they were unfortunately grounded for reasons beyond their control. But to be balled out unjustifiably in front of the ground crew by any officer, whatever their rank, was more than I was prepared to tolerate.

I was no longer a pupil pilot at school where it was to be expected, I was now a non-commissioned officer and if I conducted myself as one I insisted on being treated with the respect due to me. Certainly there were no problems on this score with the instructors. Any wigging necessary was done in private. I adopted a cavalier attitude from then on, I flew, and worked for my own esteem. Granted I had a chip on my shoulder now. Ludicrously, the incident with the controller, in my eyes, had taken first place to the much more potentially hazardous flight that led to it. No junior officer would have received such a dressing down by a senior in front of airmen, even if he was the biggest clot to ever fly. Pilot Officer Prune still existed – he was a fictitious, legendary character that never did anything right – but was never disciplined.

The instructors all thought I had put up a 'good show' regarding the forced-landing, and this mollified me coming from chaps I greatly respected. The ground crews treated me like a hero, no doubt ecstatic about the outcome of the little contretemps I had with officialdom on the runway, but it just wasn't on, as I had to tell them in no uncertain terms. I was a senior NCO I reminded them, and I did not want to hear any more flippant remarks at the officer's expense. I wasn't there to deride authority. Far from it; it was an unfortunate occurrence but I still upheld the integrity of the Royal Air Force.

The course proceeded, I took care to be above any criticism, I worked hard to prove I was a fighter pilot and thankfully succeeded in every respect. My day came when the CFI checked my progress.

We took off together to test my combat ability which meant I had to follow his every manoeuvre in line astern without losing him. It goes without saying of course that he was undoubtedly a very skilled ex-operational pilot with many combat hours in his log. He was awarded the DFC and probably hated his present job. We started off quietly, but as I stuck to his tail his aerobatics became more intricate and intrepid with his vast experience as he tried to throw me off his tail, weaving all over the sky until he blacked out in a steep turn and stalled. If I was a German he would have had it, as the saying goes, but he recovered as I circled around him ready for his next move and he called it a day; it didn't prove anything except that I was fitter and younger than he was, and could tolerate the excessive 'G' force applied. He radioed me to formate on him and headed back to base to land. His only remark at the flight hut was, 'Well done, Ashman.'

The training course came to an end, and Johnny and Mitch did exceedingly well. In the final analysis we all three passed as fighter pilots with a tremendous amount of pride and relief. We went to Cairo to celebrate and to set the town alight. Once again we were the old happy go lucky trio. Before we left we acquired a load of black market beer and sprang a party for the ground crews who had looked after us, about a dozen in all. They were both surprised and pleased; it wasn't the normal rule.

Looking back I realised that I had been extremely lucky. I was taught to fly in South Africa by first-class instructors, who were also some of the finest men I ever met socially. They had inspired me to reach my goal; they were the motivating force. We had been intimate on a man to man basis at both the schools, with no holds barred. Other pupils were not so fortunate, it was a sad sight to see failed friends leave every other week, for an obscure future. Everyone I met professionally and socially, bent over backwards to put me on the right path. Why I had this rapport in South Africa, I can't explain; it was just a plain fact, for which I was extremely grateful. It was never to be the same after that.

Here, the operational training unit instructors were first class fighter pilots and extremely good at their job too, as one would expect them to be, but they weren't interested in us as individuals. They took a purely critical point of view one way or the other. It was all in a day's work to them, as soon as they landed they expounded their views on one's aptitude and made a beeline for the mess. There was little ground instruction; they rattled off what was expected from everyone before an exercise and that was it. One either did it or made a mess of it. Success or failure was entirely in one's own hands and as a pilot they expected one to get on with it. This attitude by one's superiors, I learned later, was to be predominant for the rest of my flying service.

'The Three Musketeers' were posted to an encampment outside Almaza, a distribution centre just north of Cairo, to await our postings to operational units. We were the only three NCOs to complete the course; presumably that's why we were still together. The rest were dispersed elsewhere. We weren't aware of it then, but 1944 was the most idyllic and happiest year of all our lives. In the following year, flying in deadly earnest, sadly I never experienced the same comradeship and *jeu d'esprit* atmosphere of our training days. Those were indeed, the most wonderful times.

V

The Waiting Game

No 22 PTC (Personnel Transit Centre) was virtually deserted when 'The Musketeers' arrived by truck, on New Year's Eve, 1944. There were six sergeants in all, three from elsewhere. The vast majority of our old course were officers so it was a parting of the ways; they no doubt were sent to an officers' disposal centre. None of the usual festivities at the end of the course had been observed, not even a Xmas party; but on the other hand we had nothing in common with the other pupils. No doubt they had a rave-up in the officers' mess. The Christmas party we had organised for our ground crews and their NCOs had a much more convivial spirit I'm sure. Our little band was happy in the knowledge that our final ratings as operational fighter pilots compared more than favourably with theirs and we had no wish to be patronised. The training at Ismailia had changed us from the naive kids who left South Africa into hardened men within two months. We were confined to camp over the Christmas period to wait for our postings.

Of all the dates in the calendar to pick on, the office types chose 31 December for our posting to this transit camp. There were no more than a dozen permanent personnel in the camp including the cook. Rows upon rows of stark empty tents swayed in the winter winds (which were very cold at nights now) sited on this barren, filthy, sandy wasteland, necessitating the donning of greatcoats which hadn't seen the light of day for more than two years. It was a miserable aspect.

There was I with two Scotsmen on 'Old Year's Night' and not a drop of drink in sight. No mess open, nothing to celebrate the traditional Hogmanay with. Sacrilegious for Scotsmen. We might as well have been on the moon, the landscape in the moonlight was exactly the same; it was dead. This was the first time I'd ever seen Johnny looking so miserable, not to mention the expletives that rolled off his tongue.

Was there any wonder that we thought HQ staff were a bunch of

The author during the war.

No 8 ITW at Newquay, March to August 1943, 'B' Squadron. The author is second row from the front on the far right.

'B' Flight at No 22 Air School, Vereeniging, South Africa, April to September 1944. The author is in the back row, far left.

'Room-mates. Johnny, myself (with pipe), Gordon, Ken and Don studying a pre-flight map. Note Gordon's parrot on right arm.' Vereeniging, 1944.

'Practically a fighter, boy. Won't be long now!' Solo in a Harvard, 28 April 1944.

Outside the mess after the presentation of Wings by Field Marshal Smuts at 22 Air School, September 1944. 'Seven of the top ten of 'A' Flight: (*left*) Ken and Johnny, (*right*) Don and Gordon, (*centre at the top*) Guess who! Modesty forbids reason why.'

Hurricane replacement at No 71 OTU, Ismailia.

morons? There was no way we could get transport to Cairo; we spent a small fortune ringing up taxis to come out to fetch us but they were all busy. The stupidity of it was that we could have been given a few days' leave at our own expense, instead of being a burden to the few staff they had to retain at this god-forsaken hole. We naturally thought that we would be given leave at the end of the course anyway, especially at a holiday time. The war was far away in Italy. One sergeant was in command of the whole place. I asked him where the hell everybody was, but he was as browned off we we were. He said they were still on leave from Christmas. The camp had been cleared of people in transit before Christmas and the camp personnel sent on leave. He was unlucky to draw the short straw and we were not expected.

It was virtually the very first time that all three of us were in our beds on New Year's Eve without a smell of the stuff that cheers, trying to keep warm, fully-dressed wrapped in blankets and greatcoats. We were back to the unfeeling tradition of the service once more. I thought I had left the bad old days behind when I left the shores of Scotland. Looking at Johnny curled up in his pit muttering obscene oaths to himself as he fell asleep, had its humorous aspect and I couldn't help laughing to myself.

I could have kicked myself later when it dawned on me that I must have lost my grip, the scheming old hand had lost his touch. With my past experiences of the RAF before 1942 I should have *known* we would not have been missed if we delayed our arrival for a few days; in the old days the idea would have come to me in a flash! My disciplinary sense of duty had obviously risen to a much higher level now. With a great deal of gnashing of teeth at my stupid oversight, I told the lads that we deserved better treatment than the camp cook; in the morning we would take matters in our own hands and rectify it even though our Hogmanay would be a day late.

The next day we told the sergeant we would be unavailable for posting and telephoned a taxi from Cairo to come and pick us up. He had a fit: what was he to do if our postings arrived? We told him to forget about it, the bloody RAF would have to wait, but we would let him know if and when we returned. With that we took off by taxi to Cairo to make up for lost time and get a shave in hot water for starters. After a glorious binge we reported back the next day, keeping the taxi waiting for a quick return to town, if no orders had come through. Orders were received that very morning, putting us on standby to leave the next day, much to the relief of the sergeant; so we told him we would be back at dawn. Some of our kit left behind had been stolen; one of the numerous occasions on which this was to happen to me. The following day our posting was delayed, but we were ordered to remain at readiness for transfer to 56 PTC (Personnel Transit Camp) wherever that was. Thanking our guiding-star that we were still together, we were eventually transported by road to Abu Sueir where we embarked on a Dakota on what the crew called a milk-run. She took off for Sidi Barrani and on to Benghazi along the North African coast, picking up and putting down passengers. After an overnight stay we continued by Dakota from 512 Squadron, over the Mediterranean and up the south-eastern Italian coast to Bari, where the squadron was based. The journey was a drag in the slow Dakota, but not a safer transport aircraft ever flew.

Bari was a busy airfield and Maintenance Unit (MU). We reported our presence wondering what the next move would be. There were no fighter squadrons there, so we were at a loss to guess. The front line of that winter was a few miles north of Florence, the weather was atrocious, water pouring in torrents off the mountains filled the valleys and low-lying ground in no time at all, most of the airfields were bogged down and the Eighth Army's offensive had come to a halt. We were still unaware of where 56 PTC was, we were virtually in no man's land, nobody wanted to know us. We were given accommodation and the next day an orderly said the engineer officer at the MU wanted to see us. He had some aircraft to get off his hands he said, and asked us to air test some Spitfires Mark Vs newly arrived at the maintenance depot, which we gladly did to keep our hand in. It was a new experience to be accepted as a bona fide pilot capable of testing an aircraft's airworthiness for onward transfer to an operational squadron up north; and to sign the requisite forms. We were asked to ferry a few aircraft. I took one Spitfire to Acona (250 miles), an easy navigating trip, straight up the east coast of Italy. It was intended for 318 (Polish) Squadron then based at Forli, still flying the Mark Vc. It would be picked up by one of the squadron pilots, when one could be spared from operations presumably. I was flown back to Bari in the old Dakota transport feeling tremendously important, having made my first service flight efficiently. Our trio were kept occupied for a few days. We were immensely pleased to be treated by other pilots as part of the organisation and nobody asked how many hours we had in our log book.

A vast new experience for us was flying in winter weather. Gone were the tropical gear and sunny climes we had enjoyed for so long. We had never flown in anything but clear skies, compared with this thick nimbo-stratus cloud that reduced visibility to nil at times and tested one's instrument flying to the limit. I was glad of my training now, I never thought I would have much use for the rating 'above average'. The sudden change of climate came as a shock, we had to borrow full flying gear over our thin underwear and battle-dress, and found the cockpit was now a tight squeeze; we never thought that Italy could be so cold and wintry. This one and the previous winter were the worst Italy had experienced for years.

A few days later we were asked to fly three Hurricanes to Pomigliano, replacements for No 218 Squadron, which was flying a mixture of Warwicks and Hurricanes as an air-sea rescue unit. It was near Naples over the spine of Italy, we were told that we would not return to Bari – 56 PTC was a few miles away from Naples, our ultimate destination. The flight lieutenant of the MU unit told us that he had taken advantage of utilizing us and although we would be a week late on arrival, he had squared it with the OC 56 PTC. Our kit would follow in a transport and he was sorry he couldn't keep us, but he was killing two birds with one stone. We delivered the Hurricanes and were transported by road to this new hell of a reception centre, between Salerno and Pompeii. Everything ground to a halt as conditions worsened. We had to leave the flying suits and boots at the airfield and we were ill-equipped for the prevailing ground conditions, yet the stores would not issue us with winter underwear. 'You will get that when you join a unit,' was all the sympathy we got from the quartermaster. Our morale gradually sank, . This wasn't our scene. We expected to be up front doing a worthwhile job, and to be treated as human beings, if not as pilots.

Matters got worse: we occupied Italian villas, and the owners were thrown out; one community hall was converted into a mess for all ranks. It was back to the dark ages: the food consisted of dehydrated composite rations; literally everything was in powder form mixed with hot water to give substance. Not a can or fresh food was to be seen. I would have given a year's salary for a tin of bully beef. Officers were billeted at commandeered hotels in Naples, or

Capidichino and not stuck in this tiny village Torre El Greco, at the bottom of the slopes of Mount Vesuvius.

I felt exceedingly sorry for myself, until I saw how the Italians were living. We were scraping more off our plates than we ate, it was so unpalatable, yet young boys were dipping large empty cans into the slopbins and carrying it away for their families who thought the pig-swill a luxury; it was their main source of subsistence. A Salvation Army van traded in the piazza (square) at infrequent intervals with cups of tea and biscuits for the troops only. I bought a packet of biscuits and stood in a doorway to avoid the pouring rain to nibble away at them when I was approached by an Italian woman carrying a small babe in arms begging me for one. She chewed the hard biscuit for a while and then took small quantities from her mouth and encouraged the baby to swallow it. It was the most depressing thing I had ever witnessed. We were rationed by the Sally Army to two packets so I obtained another one and gave her it and the remains of my first packet. Her gratitude was unbelievable making me, feel extremely embarrassed. She never ate a single biscuit herself, but I didn't hold out much hope for the child if it had to rely on biscuits to live.

To my utter amazement, a woman MP (red-cap) accosted me and told me I had committed an offence by giving the Italian the biscuits. It was the first time I had seen a woman MP overseas. I told her to clear off in no uncertain terms and to stop getting her knickers in a twist. They were my biscuits, whatever I did with them was no business of hers. I never felt so incensed in all my life. I could have given her a good hiding, female or not. I wished she had been a man, I would not have hesitated to risk all to put him in hospital. She even had the confounded nerve to grab the biscuits from the woman, but I intervened. 'Accidentally' she fell on her back. Telling the mother to vamoose quickly, I made myself scarce with the help of Johnny and Mitch before this bitch of the opposite sex could whistle up reinforcements. I never felt so degraded in all my life – a RAF senior NCO treated as dirt by a woman army corporal of the military police was more than I could take. She was as livid as her red cap. Some RAF chaps standing in the piazza observed the whole incident, but one told me later that my Good Samaritan act was of no avail. Some nuns stopped the mother and child and after a few words she gave the whole packet of biscuits to them! I make no comment about that, but one can make what one will of it.

I went off alone to the local cinema in disgust, hoping for some light relief, even shunning the company of my mates. They saw the warning signs and left me to myself. I was so disillusioned with mankind, war or no war. The rain was incessant and I was glad to take shelter whatever the crummy film was.

When I came out a torrent was running down the narrow street, the drains were open and full of filth on each side of the lane. Making my way back up the hill to the billet, I was seized with gripping tummy pains, I dropped my pants in a panic but it was too late. I never felt so wretched in all my life. I'd suffered gyppy tummy in Suez, but nothing as severe as this. On arrival at the villa I stripped off outside in the pouring rain and attempted to clean my trousers under the pump. Underclothing was thrown away. I scrubbed my blue trousers on a board for hours and, soaking wet through from water above and below, I crept into the villa, naked, chilled to the bone, and climbed into my bunk. Everyone was asleep, but not for long. The charcoal fire in the middle of the room was burning hot and as the heat began to dry out my uniform, the most atrocious smell pervaded the room. In no time at all there were cries of, 'Where the hell is that foul smell coming from!'

Needless to say, I kept my head under the blankets as chaps leapt out of bed in search of the evil smell. Giving it up they got back into bed and drifted into a deep sleep. I felt wretched, but managed to fall asleep with exhaustion. The next morning I felt considerably better, the diarrhoea had cleared up and surprisingly apart from feeling washed out I was fit again. I could even see the funny side of it. I bought a pair of trousers from an airman and ditched the old ones – they were as stiff as a board. Our kit hadn't arrived from Bari, and we had no clothing excepting what we stood up in. When I told my mates they collapsed in hysterics; trust them to take the mickey. However Johnny gave me a pair of underpants; the trousers had made my backside and legs red-raw with chafing. We should have been equipped with winter flying underwear but when we attempted to obtain some, a new excuse was made. The stores hadn't any, and in any case, a bumptious stores corporal told us, we should have been equipped before leaving sunny North Africa. I demanded to know why our kit hadn't arrived from Bari. At least then we could have changed our underclothing. He couldn't have cared less, however; it wasn't his responsibility, he said. One needed to have a sense of humour at times like these, otherwise one would go bonkers or find oneself behind bars for assaulting a junior NCO.

Our morale had sunk pretty low: no flying, no future on the horizon and stuck in this dreadful place which seemed to house all the deadbeats of the RAF. Rank meant nothing here, no privileges whatsoever. It was run by a WO and a handful of senior NCOs from a tiny villa with the legend 'HQ' on the door. The administrative officers including the officer commanding were noticeably absent; there was no way of obtaining an interview with him.

However the horizon brightened considerably and the gloom lifted on the day we reported to the administrative section as usual to be told we were to join operational fighter squadrons in the north: No 111 for me; No 43 for Johnny and No 125 for Mitch. They all flew Spitfire Mark IXs and were famous units. This was fantastic news indeed for rookie pilots straight out of school; we thought we would have to put more flying time in before we were considered for operational service on a squadron. We relaxed now, trying to contain our excitement, waiting for the executive order.

We visited Pompeii to see the ruins. It was absolutely fascinating to see the remains uncovered as they were when the volcano erupted and caught everyone so unprepared. There were other things of a sexual nature that were simply amazing, phallic symbols and paintings everywhere disclosing the degenerate nature of the Romans. The baths, buildings and roads were the essence of civilisation, many years ahead of its time.

The expression 'See Naples and die' was an enigma to us. I was always under the impression that it was so beautiful it was the last place to see before one expired. It was in fact the biggest slum we had ever seen. Admittedly the war hadn't helped, but nevertheless it was a stinking hole. There was nothing to admire about the whole city; the cafés were grotty and the waiters were so dirty they put us off eating. Prostitutes abounded in every café and doorway, steeped in cheap perfume to hide the foul smell. We were pleased when our transport turned up to take us out of it.

Rome was entirely the opposite, a lovely clean city; the magnificent Coliseum, and the beautiful torrential fountains, were worth seeing but the drawback here was that it was so full of American troops, one couldn't move anywhere without being stopped by their military police. The Vatican was guarded better than the Pentagon, so we gave it up and returned to camp.

The news came through that the Fifth and Eighth Armies'

advance had stopped on the Italian front due to the appalling weather; airfields were unusable and a static situation set in. Replacement pilots were much more urgently needed on the second front where Montgomery had now established himself in Belgium after being repulsed at Arnhem. Our postings were cancelled. Before we had time to sit back and give vent to our feelings we were told we had to pack up and leave for Rome airport; we were going home.

The sequel to our sojourn in Italy was that we should never have been sent there. We should have been posted back to England; some scribe as usual hadn't done his job properly. They didn't know we existed until we turned up, so we could have stayed at Bari, or like our kit, we could have lost ourselves in any unit that wanted us.

We naturally thought that we would be flown straight home, which was now possible after southern France was occupied by the US Fifth Army joining up with the Seventh Army from Normandy. It wasn't to be: we were flown in stages by Dakota to Marseilles where we were dumped. Here again we were ignored; the transport operations from here to England were controlled and run by the Americans. No RAF transport was available. I honestly believed that we could have stayed there in Marseilles until the end of the war and no one would have been the wiser. The Yanks didn't want to know us; they were too busy getting their own troops back to England on furlough. This was one of the great differences between British and American philosophy. It never ceased to amaze me how much importance the American brass hats attached to the morale of their troops. Battle fatigue was a number one priority with them – it was as common to them as a common cold was to the British – and subsequently they were despatched to the rear and back to civilisation with the utmost alacrity. The British armed services didn't recognize this diagnosis; in the RAF it was LMF (lack of moral fibre), in other words, cowardice. What the corresponding terms were in the other services I do not know. American aircrews were only obliged to do one tour of operations before returning to the States to be fêted and receive a medal of honour, whereas the RAF minimum was two and after a rest a third tour was not unusual. Few survived that long.

The RAF administration office at Marseilles could offer no help to us, despite our official documents and orders which we carried. No RAF transport aircraft were available. We humped our gear to the airfield every day in the hopes of getting a lift through the auspices of the US Transport Command. An American technical sergeant told us that our only hope was to waylay a captain and persuade him to take us. We were not alone; hundreds of GIs milled around the tarmac with the same thought in mind. I finally got to grips with a Liberator's captain after two days. He was fully booked but he said he would take us if we got rid of our kit-bags; he was over-loaded as it was. We left them in the tender care of the RAF office never expecting to see them again, which we didn't. The Liberator was loaded up with GIs to capacity and the loadmaster said, that's all, when the captain saw us turning away for the umpteenth time. He told us to climb aboard and stand in the central aisle. Taxying to the end of the runway he opened up all four engines, and after what seemed an eternity down a very long runway, at the very end he managed to lift her off, staggering into the air at the bare minimum air speed. We didn't think he would make it. It scared the daylights out of me. It is one thing to be in charge of one's own destiny, but a different kettle of fish as a passenger. We could only hold on to the nearest seat backrest. Climbing painfully he reached his preplanned height and set course for Blighty. The aircraft was fitted out with seats similar to an airliner but the Americans occupied them and we had to stand all the way, as squatting in the aisle wasn't allowed.

It was times like this that brought home to us the iniquities of the RAF system. Oh for a commission; officers never realised the advantages they had. Here we were literally thumbing a lift home to do our duty; it was absolutely ludicrous.

Of course, when the Channel came into view we were all philanthropic towards the world in general, and the brass hats in particular. We were home, an extremely happy, wonderful feeling. Many of the chaps who left these shores wondered if they would ever see them again and history records that many didn't.

After the usual routine checking in, 'The Musketeers' were sent on a long overdue leave. Our two Scotsmen should have left for Glasgow from Euston station but they would have none of it. They were going to do me the honour of escorting me home – the long way round for them – from King's Cross. After celebrating in the city we carried crates of beer aboard the Aberdonian express that night, rousted some dudes out of a compartment and settled down to an evening of high spirits. When I disembarked at Berwick station at 4.30 a.m. we were a very subdued party, but even the after-effects of the colossal binge didn't prevent the lads from saying a rousing goodbye that scared the pigeons off the bridge and had the night foreman running about like a scalded cat. Trying to get me out of the carriage and keep them in certainly upset fellow travellers and my dignified departure. However, the porters rounded up my luggage strewn all over the platform and the train left a few minutes behind schedule with our emotions plain to see by all and sundry as they nearly fell out of the door. Somebody said something to Johnny as I ran along with the train a few yards, a flash of knuckles on bone and whoever it was, disappeared from sight. Poor soul.

Leaving the two closest friends I ever had didn't altogether blot out the euphoria of going home. Needless to say, I received the full treatment of a conquering hero, although I hadn't really been in action. My parents were immensely proud that I was a pilot, and the local newspaper that I once worked for, were not slow to interview me and write a column of local boy makes good. I was now accepted as a native of that insular town. The locomotive depot gave me a great welcome back; all the enginemen seemed to want to be part of my success because they knew how disappointed I was not to be one of them.

It felt strange to be back among the environment I loved; it hadn't changed physically but the character of the town had changed and was foreign to me – of course this was my first leave at home for two years and I found it difficult to settle. After the home-coming celebrations and meeting old acquaintances wore off, I became despondent wondering when I was going to contribute to the war effort, if at all, and what would be left for me to participate in. I found myself anxiously waiting for a telegram from the Air Ministry. I was no hero, but I was missing the active life and my pals. I was a changed person from the one that left here in 1938 and there was no way I could revert to that character. A fortnight later I was ordered to go to 7 PRC (Pilots' Reception Centre) Harrogate, to await further orders. I left home, sincerely hoping that once again, I would not be left in the wilderness of a damned disposal camp to rot.

It turned out to be a commandeered girls' private boarding school – long gone unfortunately – and the few pilots there occupied one of the dormitories; there couldn't have been more than three dozen pilots on the campus. We were the only occupants plus a small administrative staff. It was very quiet and there was absolutely nothing to do, so everyone cleared off every day to their own pursuits. I made friends with four other chaps who arrived at the same time as myself. We ate out at an inn five miles away in the countryside, walking there and back or hitching a lift where possible. We were given a subsistence allowance for this, for no cooking facilities were available at the school, merely beds. The weather was bad and when the snow began to make it hard work walking through the lanes to the pub, and the school's heating ceased to work, we decided that something had to be done about it. Half-a-dozen of us made the pub our permanent home. What else? The landlord and his wife rigged up camp beds in his two bedrooms and we moved in. We had already sampled his roast beef and Yorkshire puddings every lunch-time, but now it was bacon and eggs for breakfast, and scones for tea too, with a hot supper to end the day. This was bliss, a huge log fire in the bar and in the kitchen-cum-living room and the company of mine host, his motherly wife, and the regular farming patrons of the bar whose yarns about their lives were enthralling: poaching, game-keeping and farming. They worshipped the RAF – Yorkshire held many bomber bases – but they had little contact with them, so we were made very welcome. A telephone call to the school once a day kept us in touch with the outside world. How my old chums would have loved this environment, I missed them terribly they were always in the back of my mind.

Harrogate was a dreadfully stuffy, élite, pedantic town. One visit was enough; they didn't know or want to know if there was a war on. The upper class still came to take the spa water; it had the 'pukka sahib' colonial environment of India. Yorkshire of course is a rugged, beautiful county but we had no time to explore it; the weather was at its worst and it was covered in deep snow. If my stay there had been prolonged, I wouldn't have wanted to move anywhere. My aspiration to join a squadron was disappearing fast as nobody seemed to want me, and it began to look as though I would become some senior officer's chauffeur flying a light aircraft from base to base. This was too comfortable a billet to leave unless it was worthwhile, but all good things were bound to come to an end sooner or later.

Little did I know then I hadn't been forgotten.

VI

Called to Arms

Nicely settled in with the landlord and his family at Harrogate, living on the best country produce and sparkling ale, hemmed in with heavy snow, but comforted by a huge log fire, we received the news by telephone from the girls' school: I was posted to No 83 GSU (General Service Unit) Dunsfold.

This didn't thrill me at all, what on earth had they in store for me at a unit with a name like that, it sounded anything but promising.

Arriving in the evening, at the end of January 1945, I learnt from a chap in the mess that the station was home for many units including a pilots' conversion unit. So it would seem I was to undergo another course, and wondering what aircraft it would be, I fell into a restless sleep.

The next morning I was picked up and ushered into the presence of the OC Conversion Wing. I was delighted to be told that I was to undergo a conversion course to the latest and fastest Spitfire ever produced – the Mark XIV. This astonishing turn of events came as a complete surprise, and the immense satisfaction must have shown on my face from the way he smiled.

Within a few days I was expected to learn to fly the premier fighter of the Royal Air Force. There was a vast difference between the lower powered Mark V I had trained on at Ismailia and flown in Italy, and the Mark XIV. In comparison, it was akin to jumping from a bicycle to a 1000cc racing motor-bike in one step. My ecstasy and enthusiasm knew no bounds. The OC, a man of few words, said that tuition was virtually nil. I would be given a pilot's handbook and when I was thoroughly versed in its contents, I would be given an aeroplane to fly. He had my records but would not discuss them. All he would say was that I had come highly recommended and hoped I would live up to it, and not write off his few valuable aircraft. He only had half-a-dozen for trainees.

I went off looking for the Spitfire *par excellence* amongst neatly stacked numerous other types: Typhoons, Tempests, and Mustangs.

I was struck with awe when I came upon the flight of Spitfires sitting on their hard pad. They were distinctly the most impressive fighter I had yet seen, they had the familiar, unmistakable lines of all Spitfires but looked much more pugnacious. The much longer nose of the aircraft was filled with a huge Rolls-Royce Griffon engine with five propeller blades, compared with the smaller Rolls-Royce Merlin engine with three blades that I was accustomed to. This engine had outstripped the various updated Merlin engines to their limit; it could produce over 2,000 horse-power and attain a speed of 475 mph on the level and reach 41,000·ft. Supermarine had to build a new longer airframe to accommodate and balance this huge power unit with a modified tail-plane to balance it, mullifying the tremendous torque of the propeller shaft (for the uninitiated reader this meant that the terrific power of the engine had a tendency to twist the aeroplane like a top around the propeller shoft on its axis) instead of turning the propeller. It did look peculiar on those same little spindly legs of the earlier types.

This was the aeroplane that was designed to combat the new German turbo-jet powered, twin-engined Me262 fighter at very high altitudes. It was the only jet-powered fighter to come into operation on active service in any numbers on both sides. Our jet-powered Meteor was in its infancy and only one squadron was operational: No 616.

However, in the preceding summer when Tempests were bearing the brunt of the V1 flying-bomb onslaught, the Spitfire Mark XIV was modified, and using 150 octane fuel, raised the maximum speed to 476 mph TAS (true air speed) to combat the V1 at its low altitude of 3,000 ft. Being the newest and latest mark of Spitfire, only a few squadrons could be mustered, but they proved very successful – at all heights now, they were the supreme fighter of the RAF. Jeffrey Quill, chief test pilot for Supermarine and a serving officer, said the Mark XIV was the best fighter he had ever flown.

Considerably bucked that it was considered by the hierarchy of the RAF that my standard of flying was up to mastering and capable of taking into action this magnificent aircraft, I got stuck into the technicalities of the pilot's handbook immediately. The flight lieutenant in charge of the section was extremely helpful, but seemed dubious when he saw the few flying hours registered in my log-book. He had a good right, I suppose.

In the mess the following night, two figures strolled in. I couldn't believe my eyes. One with ginger hair and moustache and ruddy complexion, the other with curly fair hair, and a pale smooth-skinned face. They were, of course, who else but my mates Johnny and Mitch. The reunion was a boisterous affair. We had an infinite capacity to absorb punishment by way of jugs of beer, to the displeasure of the permanent staff; we certainly made the most of it.

Reporting to the OC the next morning , they presented a sorry sight, but he was no doubt used to it. They were to undergo the same five-day conversion course as myself and we had visions of eventually joining a squadron together. Pilots came and went every day here, as they completed the conversions on to different types of aircraft, or failed, whatever the case may be. Both Johnny and Mitch were as impressed with the Spitfire XIV as I was at first sight. Being a day ahead of them I was first to fly it.

I knew I had an audience as the instructor went over the details as I climbed in the cockpit which made me more nervous than ever. I could see my mates watching at the flight hut. The starting procedure differed and when the engine fired it sounded very rough, different again to the smooth Merlin, but it was obvious to me that much more power was harnessed under that huge nose. Taxying to the runway it was clumsy, forward vision was virtually nil necessitating constant swinging left and right, and sticking one's head out from one side to the other. With butterflies in my tummy I lined her up on the runway and asked permission of control to take off.

The take-off was a nightmare; to an onlooker it would appear I was a complete novice. This engine rotated the propeller the opposite way to any other Spitfire and I'd taken note of it when I read the handbook. Pilots on all aircraft have to trim the rudder for take-off to counter the torque of the propeller shaft which swings the aircraft to one side, otherwise he hasn't the strength in the opposite leg to keep it straight on the runway and the aircraft will swing off it before becoming airborne, as the power builds up. Properly trimmed, the rudder will respond to the slightest pressure of the pilot's feet. I don't know why – nerves, a hang-over or whatever – but I trimmed her for the Merlin engine as usual, the opposite to this Griffon, and opened the throttle far too wide for take-off, and too soon. I could feel the terrific thrust in my back as the speed built up much too fast; with my left foot hard down to keep her straight it was of no avail. She veered off the runway sideways, but luckily she became airborne at the wide intersection of the runways 45 degrees off course.

These Spitfires had been known to turn over on their back when too much power was applied on take-off, killing the pilot immediately. However once airborne and climbing, I pulled myself together quickly and got her under control. The power of the aircraft was fantastic. She scared me to death, she was a real handful, but I was determined to master her. Fortunately the landing was good and when I taxied back to the dispersal I got a right going over by the flight lieutenant; he said I was very lucky not have burst a tyre on take-off. Inspection of the undercarriage showed severe tyre scrub necessitating the fitting of new tyres and the oleo legs had to be checked for stress.

Later, he said he was unfair in his criticism, rechecking the records he saw I hadn't flown since leaving the Middle East nearly two months ago and that was far too long to be grounded. He thought I should have had a few refresher flights first, in an aircraft I knew, but they had no facilities for that. My old Mark V Spitfire was obsolete and he had none. Pilots ariving there were expected to go straight on to conversion courses; some on to entirely different makes. Most of them were experienced pilots from squadrons on active service or other units without any significant gaps in flying. However, he sent me up with another one that afternoon and I had no problems at all. She was so thrilling to fly, I wondered why I had made such a right cock up of it the first time.

My first flight shocked my mates as they watched me weaving about the sky like a drunken sailor battling to get the Spit under control; they didn't like what they saw. I had the reputation (undeserved in my opinion) that I was a natural pilot and they always insisted that I could fly the pants off them and 'Ashy' (my nickname) could cope with anything. Naturally I gave them the gen (information) about gently applying power to that great engine, trimming it properly for every manoeuvre and to take their time and not to panic as I obviously did. Above all, not to worry and keep off the beer; it was my fault entirely; they would have no trouble; to be forewarned was to be forearmed. They didn't look too happy about it, despite my assurances.

I needed that little contretemps with the aircraft. It deflated my ego. I was getting overconfident and conceited; being recommended for conversion to this aeroplane above others had gone to my head. I was brought down to earth from then on. I didn't put a foot wrong (excuse the pun) and pulled my finger out. She required more skill than a lighter Spitfire, to fly at low speed; but she more than made up for it when she was in full song, as all the characteristics of the earlier Spitfires made themselves apparent. Aerobatics at speed were easy if one carried them out correctly. She was so sensitive that she flicked into a spin without much warning if one was ham-handed. Once one was used to the high speed needed for the heavy all-up-weight, she was a lovely stable machine.

After only 5 hours 30 minutes' flying, I was adjudged a competent Mark XIV operational pilot to await posting to a front line fighter squadron. I must admit I thought the OC was a little premature; another 10 hours at least would have made me more confident. But I was to join a squadron having barely mastered the new aeroplane, let alone having any idea how to use it in action. I fully expected to be sent on another operational course with the new aeroplane before seeing any action, and nearly mentioned it to the OC but a sixth sense told me to keep my own counsel. To say I was confident was a blatant overstatement. I wondered why the panic to get me away, for the war seemed to be going along nicely without me. But it was a tremendous milestone for a sprog sergeant-pilot.

Unfortunately life wasn't so kind to my pals; they flew five hours and were summoned into the presence on their third day. They were told they were not up to the required standard. They were to be transferred to the Hawker Typhoon section for conversion to fighter-bombers. I should mention that each pilot was observed all the time in the air by ground observers and other instructors flying nearby to ascertain that one carried out the exercises booked to fly, and no doubt, notes were taken of one's ability; although I was never aware of their presence.

I knew that both Johnny and Mitch had difficulty in landing the Spitfire XIV when I watched them. They had narrow escapes on the approach; the necessary higher speed and side-slipping to see the runway was a manoeuvre that they got into difficulties with; but they seemed to be progressing. What other problems they had during flying, I don't know. One thing was very obvious: they didn't like this new Spitfire and thought it a brute compared with the ones we trained on. I could not argue about that; the old Mark V Spitfire was a placid bird compared with this one, but it was obvious that more powerful engines and alterations to the mainframe to accommodate that power changed many of the characteristics in the handling of the best flying machine in the world. It was a question of adjustment.

I would have entrusted my life to my mates, absolutely secure with them flying alongside me, as we did in the desert. It was very sad it was not to be. Both of them were upset with the turn of events; they were good pilots otherwise they would not have been considered as Typhoon pilots. If anything they were to follow a much more dangerous life flying these aircraft which were used as air to ground army support, shooting up anti-aircraft batteries, tanks, and heavily fortified positions in advance of the troops. They were equipped with guns, bombs and rockets for these death defying stupendous feats, the odds were tremendous; a close comparison would be the Charge of the Light Brigade at Balaclava multiplied a hundred times over.

The Typhoon belonging to the same stable as the Hurricane was a heavy aircraft and much easier to land, with good forward vision. Aerobatics were not its forte, but on touch-down it wasn't skittish; it stuck to the ground on its very wide undercarriage. It was the absolute opposite to this Spitfire, with the same narrow, spindly legs as the earlier ones but carrying a much heavier engine.

Waiting for my posting I had little to do, I watched my mates adjusting to the new type, they were coping with it very well, but to quote them, they both said, 'The Typhoon was like flying an obstreperous bus.' The finer points of flying were not required, only brute strength.

My posting orders arrived, I was to join No 130 (Punjab) Squadron based at Eindhoven, Holland. At last I was to see some action and with a crack squadron at that! I did some homework on the squadron that night with the help of the flight commander, it was their second tour on the continent since D-Day and the end of the flying-bomb campaign. They had only recently been retired back to England for a rest and had returned to Holland. There were only four squadrons equipped with the Mark XIV on the second front. Three of them, including 130, formed 125 Wing. The others were 41, 610 and 350 Squadrons. These latest Spitfires were in short supply and there was intensive competition among pilots for a posting to a squadron, so equipped.

The commander told me I was extremely fortunate to be joining 130. I was one of the few NCOs to pass through his hands to any of these squadrons, but in his opinion he thought I would cope, expressing his congratulations. I wasn't so sure but I hoped I would live up to his expectations and not make a fool of myself.

Johnny and Mitch still had to complete their flying hours on the Typhoon course so there was no means of keeping in touch with each other. They didn't know where they were bound afterwards, so we made the most of it on the eve of my departure. 'The Musketeers' had a private farewell party in the mess that night, and when the bar closed we continued in my room until the early hours. There was no doubt that my friends would fly the Typhoons and would be joining in the fray on the continent, albeit in different units and on different operations. They were in my opinion, which I was careful to keep to myself, nothing but gun-fodder, under army co-operation – expendable. Nevertheless the war was put to one side and we had a marvellous binge, reminiscing over the old happy times: such as when Mitch using live ammo missed the drogue (canvas sleeve acting as a target in the air) and nearly shot the tail off the aircraft that was towing it. That incident was proved by the evidence of the holes in the aircraft fin, and put the LAC winch operator into hospital with a nervous breakdown. Then Johnny's *faux pas* at a function in Jo'burg when – after a liberal supply of champagne I may say – he jumped on to the covered tables to entertain the guests with his version of highland dancing; only to disappear with a crash when the trestles gave way. These were but two of our many strongly disapproved activities by authority. We eventually parted, taking an oath that we would all meet again after the war. God willing.

VII

No 130 (Punjab) Squadron

Completely rekitted with a beautiful fur-lined leather Irvin flying jacket, new 'escape' flying boots, double-layer insulated underwear, a Smith and Wesson .38 revolver complete with belt and thigh holster, a pack of emergency escape rations in a flat plastic container, and a yellow Mae-West life-jacket, I was equipped for operations. The low-slung holster strapped to the thigh was found to be *in situ* for sitting in a tight cockpit. The fleece-lined black flying boots appeared to be what they were, but in fact the shoe was leather and the tops suede which could be cut or torn from the shoe to give the shoe a normal appearance. If one was shot down and survived in enemy territory and tried to make the journey back, the old type of flying boots were too obvious. Slid inside the tops of the boots was the subsistence pack containing cubes of vitamins, black chocolate, a phial of morphine with needle and a stack of blue pep-pills. One pill was guaranteed to keep one awake for 24 hours per pill – I knew this was true when by way of experimentation much later, I took one. It certainly did that and a lot more to my extreme discomfort when the effects wore off. I threw the remainder in the stove.

Waiting for the transport aircraft at the departure point, it struck me that here I was about to embark on the biggest adventure in my life. I wondered with some trepidation if in the final analysis I would be adequate and what my reception would be from the battle-experienced pilots of the squadron. I'd experienced some hairy moments merely training, but now for the first time I was to contend with people as well, whose express purpose in life was to waste all that training and lessen the strength of the air force by one, a sobering thought. Furthermore my duty would be first and foremost, to make that training worthwhile by eliminating these same people without regard to my own safety. I was going to war. Suddenly it was a reality: flying for the fun of it was finished; it had all been one big ball with my colleagues and friends.

I was a little bewildered by the speed of events: lazing about at Harrogate not ten days ago and here I was about to join a front-line fighter squadron. I only had one fear. I hoped I didn't funk it when the crucial moment arrived. I so wanted to be liked and trusted by my new companions.

Aboard a Dakota with other passengers for the continent, I was on my way to a new life. On arrival at Eindhoven, a utility truck picked me up and wended its way through a packed airfield. I was deposited unceremoniously at 130 Squadron's dispersal site and its two rickety huts which served as the office and operations room, and a pilots' rest room.

The airfield was a hive of activity: four fighter squadrons, and a few light-bomber units were based there plus various transport aircraft in a constant stream bringing in supplies for the British Second Army. Light aircraft of the Communications Flight buzzed in and out with high-ranking officers. The roar of Griffon engines greeted me as I off-loaded at the hut, sections of Spitfires were either departing for a sortie or arriving back from one. There was a purposeful air about the place that was completely new to me. The intelligence officer spotted me and dashed over to check who I was, shook hands and told me the CO was flying at the moment, and promptly vanished. I lugged my gear into the rest room and waited. Pilots came in and out of the hut giving me an inquisitive look, making me feel distinctly uncomfortable. I'd never seen such a scruffy bunch in all my life. I must have stood out like a sore thumb in my new uniform. As time went by I felt myself cringing in the corner seat out of the way, wishing I could make myself invisible.

About an hour later, there was some commotion outside as a section of Spits taxied to their parking lot and a few minutes later the figure of a squadron leader barged in, gave me a cursory glance and disappeared into his office. Hard on his heels came a bunch of pilots chattering like monkeys, flinging flying apparel all over the place as they gathered round the Spy (intelligence officer) who had reappeared from nowhere. No one took the slightest notice of me. There was a constant buzz of excitement and noisy high spirits entirely foreign to me. Everyone seemed to be competing with each other to be heard above the din and a few heated arguments broke out between individuals. Bedlam was the only word for it. I was definitely out of place here so I slid outside and had a quiet nervous smoke sitting on a wooden bench. The pilots gradually came out and dispersed to the mess.

A voice from within bellowed, 'Where the hell is this new man?'

Promptly throwing the cigarette away I nipped through the doorway to be confronted by the squadron leader I had seen come in, the commanding officer of 130 Squadron, Squadron Leader M.R.D. Hume, DFC (a New Zealander) who beckoned me into his office with a curt wave of his hand. He sat and read through my records and log-book, studied the log-book again whilst I fidgeted. Then looking me straight in the eyes, he said with some venom:

'How in God's name, did you ever get yourself posted to this squadron?'

Taken aback, feeling my face go a deep red, I mumbled, 'Orders, sir.'

'This is ridiculous,' he yelled. 'What the hell will they send us next? We badly need experienced pilots and look what we get! A sergeant straight out of school and still wet behind the ears.' He was furious, as he went on, 'I suppose after 5 hours 30 minutes on our Spits (referring to the Mark XIV) you think you're an ace.' Well, what could I say to this character? I was bursting to tell him to go to hell after my initial discomfort. Instead I asked permission to leave his office. He sat back looking at me and in a calmer voice he said, 'Sorry about that. It's not your fault but the situation is preposterous. We will leave it on the table for now.'

I'd been interviewed by more senior officers than a squadron leader in the past and with some bravado I had more than held my own in the interchanges, but this chap in his worn, frayed uniform and ragged, peaked cap had much more stature than any brass-hats I ever met. He was the boss and there was little I could say. He summoned a corporal clerk and told him to show me the mess and living quarters and give a hand with my gear.

'Report back in the morning,' were his parting words.

A thoroughly dejected pilot was led away much to the amusement of the corporal who said out of hearing, 'Don't let it worry you, Sarge. His bark is worse than his bite and if he didn't like the look of you, your gear would have been left in the office for you to collect in the morning, on your way back to wherever you came from. I've seen some chaps get off a transport from the UK in the morning and go back the same day.'

I was ready to grasp any straw and I thanked him for the moral support.

The living quarters held two to a room. I was ushered into a room with one occupant: he was Warrant Officer Mike Ockendon. He was flat out on his bed reading a book and looking up, he said, 'Hello, old man, make yourself comfortable.'

With that he carried on reading as though people came and went all the time, it was so matter of fact. The bed was already made up and as I unpacked a few things in silence I was dying to introduce myself, and ask him what the normal course of events was for a new man. But I was afraid to interrupt his reading as he himself made no effort to converse. I thought it was a very odd situation and one I hadn't come across before.

I wrote a few words in my diary just to pass the time until he rose from his bed and said, 'Dinner time, you coming?' Dinner time on the squadron was in the evening, and the old midday dinner was lunch. As an afterthought he said, 'I'm Mike.' He joined five NCO pilots at a table, noting two other WOs and three flight sergeants. He said to the others, 'Meet my new room mate.' With that, they looked up from their conversation and nodded. During the meal they chatted amongst themselves, I felt out of my depth in this company, there was nothing I could chip in with, and if I did, I had a feeling they were waiting to hear me 'shoot a line'.

I had an inferiority complex with the day's events, I was asking myself if I was in the same Air Force that I had known for all these years. Where was all the squadron camaraderie I had heard so much about? It was so embarrassing to sit eating in silence out on a limb, so I hurriedly finished my meal and left.

When Mike showed up two hours later, I was in bed thinking about the morrow and what lay ahead, I wasn't all that sure I wanted to stay now even if the CO accepted me. I was pretty browned off with this shower, I did expect to be made welcome and at least have a drink in the bar. It had been a tiring day. Mike got the message by my brusque attitude, he said, 'Sorry about that, mate.' (An admission he knew why I was browned off.) 'You're not on the pay-roll of the squadron yet but when you are, things will change, you'll see. We have had so many potential chaps who decided after a short stay with the squadron to transfer to another unit, because they couldn't cope or lost their nerve, so every new arrival is treated with suspicion until the boys know he can be trusted.' I said I supposed the fact that I was an inexperienced sergeant had a lot to do with it. 'Not at all,' he said. 'You are the first new sergeant to join the squadron in our time, but you'd be surprised at the number of more senior chaps than you who went back to the jobs they had before.'

I muttered with my head in the pillow, 'I'm not surprised,

goodnight,' at which he laughed and said, 'You'll be ok, mate,' as he hit the sack.

The next morning, breakfast was a hurried affair. One section of four aircraft had already taken off. I sat outside the dispersal hut twiddling my thumbs, until a clerk called me and told me to collect a chute from the stores, be ready to take off in 15 minutes, and not to be late. At my quizzical glance he said the CO was taking me up. I shot off to collect the chute and dashed around the dispersal looking for AP–N and finally found it hidden behind a blast-wall a good 150 yards away. Lugging a parachute and harness around is heavy work; the chute was the fighter pilot's seat which fitted into the steel recess and backrest, with only a hard pad or a packed deflated dingy between one's backside and the chute. Waving to the ground crew to strap me in, I wedged myself in the seat and went through the checks in a flash, as the crew kindly gave me some advice about that particular Spitfire. I couldn't see the CO start up so I waited until one of the lads gave me the signal to start up. Fortunately she fired first time, running up the engine and completing more checks, I taxied out to the track to see the CO's aircraft disappearing at a rate of knots along the rough winding taxi-track. Panic set in as I went hell for leather after him to catch up before he reached the runway. He was asking permission from control to move on to the runway when I reached him.

Quickly going through the pre-flight checks I stationed myself in echelon: slightly behind and to the right of him for a formation take-off. With a wave of his hand he opened up and watching him like a hawk I stuck to him like glue as we tore down the runway a wing's length away. From the steep, tight climbing turn to the left, until our return he gave me the works.

I thought the instructors at OTU were good, but they were novices compared with this chap. We chased each other, going through every manoeuvre in the book until completely exhausted, as he sat on my tail for the umpteenth time, I was glad when he called it a day and we returned to base. It dawned on me that, if he had been a German I would have had no chance with anyone of his ability, and I was under the impression all German pilots were. Luckily that was a fallacy.

It was a cold day, and I wore nothing but my battle-dress, but I was wringing wet with perspiration when I climbed out of the kite. An armourer asked, with a grin, 'How did it go, Sarge?' I gave him a withering look; he was trying it on, and I wasn't going to give him any fodder for gossip amongst his mates. One had to be respected otherwise they would take advantage in the future.

Staggering back to the rest-room, I was told that the CO would see me shortly. The place was a hive of activity again with the roar of engines starting up and pilots coming and going in and out of the ops room; I was alone in the rest-room restlessly pacing up and down and smoking my head off as the time dragged by. The longer I waited the more I thought that I would be sent packing, back to the UK. The CO was constantly dashing in and out of his office, completely ignoring me, until with a wave of his hand he beckoned me to follow him inside and told to shut the door after me. Anticipating the worst I stood ready to take it.

He told me to pull up a chair and sit. He seemed in a much better mood than yesterday, cool, calm and collected. He is going to let me down softly was the thought that ran through my mind. Glancing at a sheet of paper in front of him, he said he had formed his judgement: my standard of flying was quite good, airmanship excellent, but a typical product of first-class training by the book. He admitted that I had natural talent and advised me to apply it and forget the book. Having said that, he went on to say that it left a lot to be desired, which would only come by experience the hard way. He said if I chose to remain with the squadron, I could not expect to be nursed although he would do his best to keep me out of trouble in the early stages. I must be keen otherwise I would not be there, but he did not want anyone on his squadron who thought it would be a picnic. I would have to take my chances.

He would leave it up to me and give me time to think it over. In his opinion I should not be there until I had amassed more flying hours on an advanced flying unit. I could apply for a transfer and it wouldn't be held against me by anyone in the RAF. There were plenty of other jobs that needed a good pilot and if I thought my inexperience was detrimental to putting up a first rate job on the front-line, I just had to say so.

He had me in over a barrel, I wondered if it was a ploy to test me or get rid of me, his face was impassive. Come back tomorrow and let me know how you feel about it were his parting words.

With a sudden rush of blood to the head I thought I would call his bluff and blurted out, 'I'll be glad to join the squadron, sir, if you think I'll make the grade.'

He stood up, extending his hand and with a smile. He said, 'Welcome to 130 Squadron, sergeant. That's what I wanted to hear.' He dismissed me with a wave of his hand. Smartly saluting him, I strode out of the office like a dog with two tails, morale lifted and confidence restored.

All I had to do now was win over my fellow pilots. As far as the NCO pilots were concerned I needn't have worried, the grapevine soon went into action and when I went into the mess that night they all shook hands. The boss was obviously held in high esteem and if one was good enough for him, one was accepted by all the pilots. Of course there was a long road ahead and I had yet to prove to have what it takes on my first few operational flights with them before I was accepted as one of them. They now knew I could fly but could I fight? It all depended on the circumstances, and opportunities that presented themselves to gain their full confidence.

I learnt that the squadron was a mixed colonial and British unit. Normally officers made up two-thirds of it and the NCO complement were: Warrant Officer Mike Ockendon; Warrant Officer Mick Coverdale; Warrant Officer Jim Boulton (Australian); Flight Sergeant Bert Woodman (New Zealander); Flight Sergeant Phil Clay and A.N. Other Flight Sergeant.

However, it appeared they had been through a bad time just prior to my arrival and in addition to war losses, a number of officer pilots were tour expired and rested: the last two Canadian pilots had gone home. The full complement of the squadron was 18 pilots and 18 aircraft (six of which were spares). Mike told me they were down to 14 fit pilots at that moment.

That afternoon Sergeant Pilot George Warren arrived. He was a day late and came from Dunsfold where I had flown my conversion course. Surprisingly we hadn't met, although I thought I knew all the few Spitfire pilots there. However, it seems he had been around some time in Britain, he was trained in Canada and it amazed me to learn there were numerous spare bods not flying on operations. I've no knowledge of his record but the CO accepted him with little fuss. He seemed to know the drill but had little to say.

We brought the NCO complement up to seven, taking the places of two officers, Flight Lieutenant Matheson and Flying Officer Martin who left the day before.

That night a flight lieutenant breezed into the bar and made a beeline for our party. 'You are Ashman?' he asked. When I replied in the affirmative, he went on, 'Report to me 0900 hours for formation flying. You will see the details on the board in the ops room.' With that he turned on his heel and went. Mystified, I asked Mike what that was all about, he said that the officer was Flight Lieutenant Walmsley, 'B' Flight commander and it looked as though I was assigned to his flight. He said not to worry, he probably wanted to look at my formation flying in a section and correct any faults before starting the real work.

Two flights made up a squadron, but they never flew as such, it was mainly to distribute the ground work evenly between the flight commanders, and take the administration of everyday paper work off the CO.

In the morning I saw I was down to fly in a section of four led by Flight Lieutenant Walmsley, I was his wingman (No 2): Flying Officer Stott on the other side of him was No 3 and his wingman (No 4) was Sergeant George Warren. The leader briefed us about keeping station on each other in the 'finger-four' formation and how imperative it was to rigidly adhere to it. It was purely an exercise to see how George and I shaped up. The finger-four formation is explained by placing one's left hand on a table hiding the thumb and looking at the position of the four finger nails, substituting the nails for aircraft. Only used by fighters, it was always referred to as 'battle formation'. Three sections of four, formed a squadron, with the leading one slightly ahead of the other two on each side of him.

I thoroughly enjoyed the exercise; the section banked, turned, dived and climbed as one as the leader weaved around the sky. Formation flying was my forte so I was very happy when the weather closed in and the leader told us to close up on our way back to base. Tucking my port wing just behind his starboard wing was a bit too much for him, it made him nervous, he called out, 'Red two, you'll be in my lap in a minute.' His report to the boss must have been favourable, he had no criticism to make about us, and I flew as No 2 thereafter with the boss and other section leaders. The prime duty of a No 2 was to safeguard the rear of the leader when he made his attacks and prevent an enemy fighter getting on his tail, so he could devote all his concentration on whatever he was attacking. This enemy manoeuvre from a greater height and from behind was called 'bouncing'. The best leaders could look after themselves and even had time to keep an eye on their wingman (No 2) in case he also ran into trouble in a mêlée. Nonetheless, history records a number of aces including Douglas Bader who came to grief when their wingman was otherwise engaged.

After a lone sector reconnaissance to get the lie of the land, my name was added to the list of operational pilots chalked up on the squadron's personnel blackboard. I had arrived.

The strength of the squadron was now 16 officers and 8 NCOs. Flight Lieutenant Earp and Flying Officer Heale had gone missing, but by the end of the month six replacements had arrived; three officers, Warrant Officer Andy Miller from 41 Squadron, myself and George. The officers came from the disbanded 610 Squadron, consequently all the replacements excepting George and myself were very experienced combat pilots in our mark of Spitfire. No doubt the boss was extremely pleased about that.

The CO led the whole squadron in an exercise shortly afterwards to fit the new men in. One trip of 55 minutes was totally inadequate of course but he chivied everyone into some semblance of a fighting unit in squadron formation; he could at least lead 12 aircraft into action, whatever the result. He seemed satisfied with the exercise. I realised now what a responsible job he had, and understood his irascibility when a sprog like me turned up. In fact he was a mild-mannered man, and a born leader. I never heard him raise his voice again unless he was badly let down. Thank goodness I personally never gave him any further cause. He had the utmost respect for his NCOs as men and as pilots. His attitude was the same to all the ground crews and their NCOs. Rank did not sway him. He was the boss, the managing director of the firm. Seldom did he have recourse to take any of the men to task and discipline them; they never murmured when asked to work long hours to repair aircraft and make them serviceable in dreadful conditions due to the weather. He had the charisma to get the best out of everyone on the ground and in the air. I grew to like him tremendously.

Going back a month, to explain the stage of the war in February to put this narrative in perspective: The disastrous Arnhem assault by the 1st Airborne Division and the British Second Army had faded as had the Battle of the Bulge, the surprise German offensive in the Ardennes. Now the Allied armies were pushing forward to the Rhine. The Second Army was holding the enemy counter-attacks on a broad front at Nijmegen ten miles to the north of our base at Eindhoven. The weather was atrocious, and both sides were bogged down, flying operations were limited due to the poor visibility and the low-lying airfields alongside the river Meuse were under water. Medium-bomber raids from East Anglia and heavy bombing by US Eighth Air Force and Bomber Command were unaffected but the 2nd Tactical Air Force under whose auspices we operated, and based on the continent, were at a distinct disadvantage. Montgomery at Brussels built up his logistics whilst the army consolidated their positions behind the Vaal and the Maas, and he was now on the advance pushing the Germans back behind the Meuse where they were dug in.

My very first operational flight was three days after my arrival. Our briefing was to escort American Mitchell medium-bombers over the Ruhr and turn north to Borken. The formation of bombers was called a 'box' and required a whole squadron of 12 aircraft as cover. We took off and met the bombers at the assigned position as they crossed the Dutch coast and took station on them above and behind. I was the CO's wingman. No enemy fighters showed up and we had a comfortable trip in comparison with the bombers below. They got on with their job, but encountered heavy flak from medium-range A/A batteries. Some 88mm guns opened up on us. It was my baptism to enemy fire, and seemed very strange, so unreal; puffs of smoke were everywhere but I felt completely detached as it was noiseless of course. The roar of the engine drowned the explosion unless a shell scored a hit. I got a fright when one exploded between me and the boss. I couldn't see him for a second, as the smoke blotted him out and I wasn't to know he hadn't been hit. However, all was well. The boss showed no concern and never deviated from his course.

The batteries concentrated on the Mitchells with 37mm guns as they reduced height. It was a wonderful sight to see the pyrotechnic display of tracers of all colours criss-crossing until suddenly one bomber trailed smoke and went into a spiral dive. It seemed an eternity before a flash on the ground obliterated him; the pyrotechnics didn't appeal to my sense of beauty after that. It was the only glimpse I had of anyone being shot down. I was too busy scanning the sky for 'bandits' in the odd moments I dared take my eyes off the boss. We saw them safely on their way home, but how many there were I've no idea. The result of the raid remained unknown, the log read DCO (duty carried out) which made it hard for a diarist – not that I was one. In fact I was very dilatory in keeping my log-book up-to-date as time went by, and a clerk constantly chased me about it. I had a habit of leaving entries for a few days and consequently there are a number of flights not recorded at all when it was mislaid. These days I didn't attach much importance to it. I was lazy; at training schools it was strictly enforced and had to tally with the record clerks. Details entered in one's own log were frowned upon I was told, so one had to be content to record the bare facts. Not that there was much room for anything else in it. Sometimes the duty in the authorisation book was so obscure, I didn't know exactly where we were going except to a certain area. Of course a flying log-book is only meant to record one's flying hours.

My next trip was a little solo jaunt. I was detailed to collect a new Spitfire XIVe from Dunsfold and fly it back to base. Presumably I was the messenger boy being the newest, so I couldn't grumble. An Anson communications aircraft picked me up for the two-hour flight back to England and on arrival I was told by the Maintenance Unit's CO I would have to stay overnight. When I was shown the station sergeant's mess and a room to myself in it, I didn't object. When I was there before on the conversion course the mess set aside for itinerants was sub-standard. This mess was the best I'd ever been in, waited upon hand and foot by WAAF stewardesses I was loath to leave it. I gave the aircraft allocated to me an air-test first thing in the morning, but turned it down. It had a fault on the automatic propeller pitch control. So I had to wait until after lunch whilst the Engineering Officer sorted out another one. Having tested this one, I was delighted with her performance and decided not to delay any longer and told the OC that I would leave at 1500 hours. The weather had been fine all day but the met office told me a front was building up over the North Sea and advised against it. I felt I must get away from this luxury or I may never go back. The previous evening I had a jolly time at a local pub, in the company of my own kind and arrived back legless. The war seemed far away from here.

This Spitfire was a beauty, fitted with the latest cockpit and a pear-drop canopy which gave one an unimpeded view all round – it was like sitting in a perspex globe – and even a cockpit heating system. We took off and set course for Eindhoven in good conditions. The note of the engine was the smoothest I'd ever flown, and she was a pleasure to fly. Nearly 25 minutes later the Channel came into view on my starboard (right) side and the weather worsened. Banks of cloud lay dead ahead. This must be the front I thought, steadily climbing I lost sight of the Channel and the Straits of Dover directly ahead as I tried to get above it, flying on instruments I cleared the clag at 29,000 ft. The direct course I was steering was over the North Sea at an angle, and I had to guess when I had crossed. The only way to fix my position was to drop down through the dense cloud and hope that the base of it wasn't at ground level!

Suddenly silver shapes slid by. My God, I thought, I'm in the middle of a balloon barrage! The altimeter read 5,000 ft; they must be at half-mast or above. Giving her the gun, I climbed like a bat out of hell. She responded marvellously as I weaved about, when a balloon loomed up directly ahead. I was having kittens. My main worry was fear of colliding with an unseen cable tethered to a balloon above me which would have cut the aircraft in two, I didn't like the idea one little bit, there would be hell on if I lost a brand new aeroplane on my first important assignment on the squadron; not to mention the dire unknown consequences to me physically if I survived baling out. I didn't fancy being strung up by the parachute strings on a church spire or going through someone's glass roof. In actual fact I was blown 20 miles off course and should have made landfall south of Ostende. The timing was right but the course well out. Nobody had briefed me that balloons were in use on the continent so I guessed it could only be Brussels. It was.

However all was well as we reached the blue sky above again. I was disoriented, a blanket of cloud lay below me in all directions, but I knew that Eindhoven was roughly 65 miles north-east of Brussels. A voice in my headphones startled me. The American accent said, 'You are in a prohibited zone. Please identify yourself.' I had to laugh, he was telling me! Of course the device fitted to all RAF aircraft which identified one as a friend or foe by radar was switched on. I gave him the details he asked for and requested a course to steer for base – I had no means of determining the wind strength and was only equipped for map reading. As I circled around, the voice came back giving a course to steer for Eindhoven.

Setting course, he kept in touch until I was over base. I thanked him for his assistance and switched over to the frequency of Eindhoven's controller. The problem now was to let down 28,000 feet through thick cloud and hope to see the airfield. I was told the base of it was 800 ft so I had nothing to worry about. Once under the base of the cloud I soon found the airfield, not a mile away. About 15 minutes late on ETA.

Safely landing, I reflected that it was the longest trip I had flown by compass alone. In fact it was the longest distance I had ever flown solo – about 315 miles and not without incident. I was a happy man as I taxied back to the dispersal. Flying time 1 hour 40 minutes.

Reporting to the boss of the delivery of one brand new Spitfire No MV268, he seemed pleased to see me but he merely asked, 'Have a good trip?'

'Yes thank you, sir,' I replied, wondering uncomfortably how much he knew.

'Good show, Ashman. The weather's been rather duff and we haven't got one aircraft off the deck today. Go and get your tea and put your feet up.'

He was obviously aware of the conditions of the trip, as control would have kept him informed, but he gave no indication of it. He was impassive. That particular aircraft was the first and last of the modified Mark XIVe I ever saw, the rest of the production were shipped overseas to India and Burma. No doubt MV268 was snapped up by a brass-hat after some of the boys had tried her out. She never bore 130 Squadron's identification letters of AP which would normally be painted on her, and I never saw her again.

As Field Marshal Montgomery pushed forward at a rapid rate, the squadron was kept busy on armed reconnaissances ahead of the British Second Army. This entailed attacking railheads, ammunition and troop trains, road convoys, armoured cars and mobile artillery batteries – everything that moved was stopped. This was the ground-attack role of the squadron. We had two 20mm Hispano cannons firing tracer, armour-piercing, and explosive shells which could do a great deal of damage to semi-armoured vehicles and locomotives. We were operating in sections of eight or as a full squadron.

The first attack I ever made was on a marshalling yard. It was also the first low-flying exercise I had flown since training days when we only had the Browning .303 machine guns; they were very lightweight compared with the cannons. This mark of Spit also had a new gyro gun-sight I was unacquainted with; I opened fire on a signal box and was amazed at the recoil of the cannons which altered the trim of the aircraft in a dive. I couldn't get the correct deflection on the sights and the shooting was off line. What a mug I was. I realised then that there was a lot of work to catch up on that had never occurred to me before. I hit the signal box (my God it was big enough!) but I didn't fancy my chances with anything that moved! I strafed some vans. Luckily they were all coupled together because the ones I aimed at went unscathed but the others got the full treatment. I was extremely happy not to meet any Luftwaffe fighters over the next few days, a deadly dedicated enemy pilot would have made mincemeat of me if the flak didn't beat him to it. The results didn't look too bad on film, but they didn't know what I did. It was imperative I spent more time studying the gun-sight on the ground and working out the amount of trim needed in a dive at different speeds to keep the aircraft steady. The aircraft was supposed to be a flying gun platform, therefore trimming it to fly with hands off in any attitude was paramount. Hands off, is a bit of an overstatement of course. There were times I asked myself what the hell was I doing here. I seemed to have forgotten all I had ever learnt, I felt such a useless clot.

Gradually I got used to the flak. It had to be ignored if an attack was to be pressed home. Fortunately damage to my aeroplanes was superficial; a few bent and holed panels and a burst tyre on one occasion, but nothing to worry about: they all flew again.

I felt I was making progress. After all, I only had ten hours' flying time including those at Dunsfold on this type, and it would take time given the chance, to master this aircraft as a fighting machine. When one went into action it was sudden, reaction had to be extremely fast to force the aircraft into position and make it obey one's commands instantly. An entirely different situation to zooming around the sky at leisure for one's pleasure.

The CO was evidently satisfied with the way I was shaping, but he said he thought I was too much of a perfectionist. My flying was OK, I had a natural aptitude but I was still trying to fly by the book. I should adapt it to wartime conditions and relax more. 'Forget the training manual. You are concentrating on keeping station to within a few yards as though it was a flying display which you do admirably, but in so doing you are not twisting your head around. You must keep a sharper look-out.' He added that he thought I would make an operational pilot with more experience. I mentioned I hadn't met any opposition yet. He said not to worry, and not to be so anxious; it would come. The longer I lived the more experienced I would become. Big joke. That was an understatement if ever there was one.

In the Battle of Britain days so long ago, there was no option. Young newly fledged pilots with no experience had to get stuck in and suffered the consequences by losing their lives, except the few fortunate or lucky – or astute characters who collected gongs – in a very short period of time. This was a different war, different tactics, and different aircraft; there was more time to spare for training. Little is heard today of the majority who died without any fuss.

In retrospect I wondered why as late as 1945, raw pilots were not trained in the latest combat tactics on the latest fighter aircraft, before they were thrown in the deep end. The training methods were outdated as I discovered too late in the day, success didn't depend on one's prowess at performing standard aerobatics, quite the contrary; they were seldom used in combat. It was much more important to be able to do a tighter turn than the foe in attack or defence. No one on the squadron bothered to advise, instruct or discuss flying tactics. I quickly discovered that if one was posted to a squadron and accepted, one was expected by the rest of the squadron to know it all! The blasé instructions given in the comfort of the briefing room before a sortie were so different when the time came to carry them out – it was a foregone conclusion that they would be carried out – it was so easy! One daren't ask any questions, in fear of drawing everyone's attention and made to look foolish.

It appeared to me that these short briefings were a waste of time, the officers seemed to be clued up beforehand and probably had it all worked out in the mess the night before. They knew the battle zone like the back of their hand, the hunting grounds had been covered many times. Memories were short. If we lost a pilot, it was quickly forgotten unless he was particularly well-known. Changing personnel obviated close contact. This isn't a narrative of the exploits of the squadron as a whole, but of people whom I lived and worked with – there were pilots whose acquaintance I never made. It would be impossible to give a blow by blow account of everyone. One only knew what happened in one's own particular section on a particular sortie, and when operating in larger formations – as a whole squadron. Operations were not a general topic amongst us at any time.

At this early stage, I wondered if I would have been happier on a photo-reconnaissance unit, flying the sister Spitfire Mark XIX, but with a longer range and equally as fast especially at high-altitude. These squadrons flew as individuals, one aircraft, one man. Operations were photographing enemy installations, concentrations, and the results of bombing operations. I felt I would have been of more value as my own master, with a specific duty to do. I always

'Mitch and myself at the Christmas party, Ismailia. Johnny took the photo.'

Hurricanes at Ismailia, November 1944. 'Getting ready for the day's work with these lovely machines and chatting with the bods responsible for our "welfare".'

Top 'Good drinkers all!' Author is third from the left. Ismailia, 1944.

Above 'Mitch and myself (*right*) with a guide outside a tomb near Cairo. Johnny took the photograph.'

Left The author with a Spitfire.

Top right 'A South African pal of mine, Jan Smidt.'

Above right 'Peace and quiet at the end of the day.' The Spitfire flight line at Ismailia.

Right 'Awaiting final assessment by CFI, 29 November. Fingers crossed!'

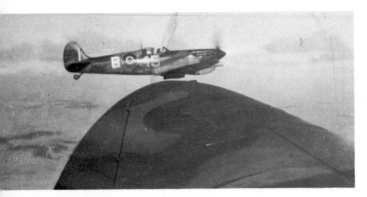

With the Air Firing Squadron in December 1944. 'Made it at last!'

Formation returning after gunnery high over the desert near Suez. 'This is the life.'

'The Three Musketeers. Mitch, myself and Johnny Dick in the happy days.'

loved flying alone to do my own thing and enjoyed putting the aircraft through its paces, when the mood took me. I had every confidence in my navigation and disliked the herd atmosphere of the fighter squadron, where one just followed the leader and had no idea of where one was, or where one was going. Photo-recce was a dangerous job but one had to look out for oneself. All things being equal I was sure I could give a good account of myself. I dismissed the idea because I didn't know how to approach the boss. For the life of me I didn't want to get on the wrong side of him; he would want to know why.

The NCOs had little contact with the officers except when flying, at briefing sessions and sitting around waiting at the dispersal. Everyone depended to a certain extent on the other; incongruously the three warrant officers led sections of four Spitfires on sorties on odd occasions, including officers in the section. They took it all as a matter of course, they were experienced combat pilots. If they were in command it made no difference what rank the officers held, they did their job and expected the others to carry out their orders. Once on the ground the positions were reversed, but that didn't prevent them giving a new flight lieutenant in their section a dressing down for some sloppy flying, but that was the end of the matter.

NCOs never flew together as a single section; generally a section of four was made up of one NCO and three officers. Consequently after a sortie, the NCO was isolated when flying was finished and the officers were not inclined to discuss it with him, unless he deserved congratulations.

I didn't know if it was a unique characteristic of 130 Squadron, but all my service life I was under the impression that pilots of any squadron whatever the rank had a strong comradeship within the unit. Certainly esprit-de-corps was prevalent in the whole of the RAFF's other ranks on any station, but whereas it existed in 130Squadron too, to a certain extent; the squadron's pilots were intrinsically individualists. Officers in the main stuck together, which was understandable, but to my surprise the NCO pilots hadn't any bond amongst themselves. George was almost always preoccupied reading books in his room in the evenings. Phil, a brilliant pilot, undoubtedly the ace NCO, had unusual tendencies. Having a room to himself – nobody would share it with him – for amusement, he lay in bed shooting at flies on the ceiling with his revolver, or throwing darts if ammunition was low. He was a very restless chap, never happy unless he was flying and always wandering around the maintenance echelon (130's ground crew) unit flinging spanners about and making himself a general nuisance to NCO's in charge. He had no outside interests; he only lived to kill Germans and he didn't know the word fear. His one aim in life was to increase his score. Mike on the other hand was a married man with a family, very much so, writing pages and pages to her every night; the last thing he did before turning in was to post the letter. All of them were about my age of 24 or older. George was the youngest, Mike was the eldest. I had no hobbies at hand, or close family or romantic connections to relieve the everyday tensions.

None of the NCOs seemed to have anything in common; they preferred their own company as a general rule in off duty hours, staying in their rooms apart from mealtimes and occasional visits to the bar. Of their personal lives I learnt nothing in the whole of my time with the squadron. I was prepared to satisfy anyone's curiosity about me if they were interested merely for the sake of conversation, but none wanted to know. Mike was no trouble to share a room with; we got on very well together. He was the most easy-going chap I ever met but there was always that barrier that prevented me asking personal questions. He kept his distance, never mentioned his family, never showed me his family photographs. The same applied to them all and I wasn't used to it. I was definitely the odd man out, maybe because I was the only unmarried one, maybe I never took life seriously on the ground, or possibly I was too high-spirited. They were friendly enough of course, making the odd wise-cracks, but conversation was mundane at the dispersal and at mealtimes. Socially they were far too serious for me, seldom letting their hair down. I was living in the past, rapidly coming to the conclusion that I had been reading too many press reports of the happy-go-lucky, carefree, nonchalant fighter pilot's life.

I had hoped that these chaps would give me the valuable information I desperately needed, to enable me to play a full part in action, but as it wasn't forthcoming my pride prevented me from asking and I made my mind up not to be so timid and subservient. The halcyon days of South Africa and the Middle East had gone forever and I missed the sky-larking and comradeship of my old mates very much indeed. There was probably a good reason for the blasé, phlegmatic attitude of my new comrades.

Micky, Mike, George and Bert seldom frequented the bar as a party, they drifted into the mess individually for a quiet pint. If the general public got the impression from the press that every night was one long binge, they were sadly mistaken. Phil, too, often kept to his room. It was rare for all of us to drink together so I joined the Typhoon pilots, in the evenings, enjoying the company and high spirits of these chaps. It was too risky to over-indulge, but at least for a little while it took one out of oneself and lifted the odd bouts of depression caused by the atmosphere of my new comrades. In fairness to my new squadron comrades, I may have been too exuberant and possibly their self-assurance was a façade to overcome their own inadequacies and fears. At this stage I didn't give much thought to living or dying if it comes to that. I lived for the day.

The junior officers were very fair, I was accepted by them as a fellow pilot and their companionship was appreciated at dispersal and on the very odd occasions we had a drink together. Except for a few, ex-instructors from Canada who had difficulty forgetting the bull out there, the junior officers disregarded the formalities of rank and treated the NCOs as one of them whilst they were flying. Each pilot at some stage was dependent on the others to pull them out of a sticky position; similarly we all depended on the grounds crews to have the aircraft in first-class operating condition. The crews who looked after our Spitfires were happy-go-lucky chaps, they worked like beavers to get the aircraft serviceable, sometimes all through the night after putting in a day's work. If the guns had been fired they wanted to know every detail: played hell if there was a hole or a dent in a panel and moaned about the extra work of replacing them. In mock indignation they complained of their beautiful aircraft being badly treated. If a gun had jammed, it was no use balling the armourer out: he was just as upset as the rest of us. I envied Mike, because he had his own personal aircraft, and was often seen in the evenings cleaning it. I hadn't reached that stage.

Generally, squadrons worked up together in a rest period away from the front line, and faulty flying and tactics perfected until the whole squadron worked as a team. There was no comparison to the training I had received in 37 flying hours at the training unit in the Middle East, to the real thing. It was entirely different to what I expected. It was one thing to practise tactical attacking set-pieces among fellow pupils, when a mistake was of no account, but it was entirely different when none of it seemed applicable here. This was for real; it was apparent to me that the squadron were fielding their first team in the first division, but a few of us needed time to fit in with the team's tactics. There was no doubt the majority were well trained in fighter tactics and in ground attacking roles: taking their place in the squadron with some aplomb and confidence.

I hung on, grappling with the situation, outwardly I hoped I gave the impression I was competent, but inwardly I wasn't sure of myself at all. Flying was a piece of cake but without someone taking the trouble to give me a thorough grounding on tactics, I was at a loss as to what was expected of me, for quite some time. I developed into a split personality, I wanted to be my natural inherent self and not give a damn about anything or anyone, but my training and professionalism would not allow me to do so. Consequently I had this worry for the rest of my flying career whilst on operations but I kept it carefully hidden from any outside observer. I had this horror of letting the side down and possibly being held responsible for some untoward incident with disastrous results, despite what the boss had said. I witnessed some nasty scenes between him and an officer who had put someone in jeopardy. I had to subdue my natural instincts, no matter how I felt.

When I was successfully converted to the top fighter of the day in only five-and-a-half flying hours at Dunsfold, my ego knew no bounds. I was immensely proud of the fact that I alone, out of 50 pupils who gained their wings with me at 22 Air School, achieved operational status on this superior type of Spitfire; even surpassing the skilful abilities of my closest friends at Ismailia. I could only guess that the CO there had something to do with it, fulfilling his promise. However, joining a real operational squadron had brought me down to earth with a bump and knocked any pretentious or grandiose ideas right out of my head. The only records that mattered here were how proficient one was in combatting the enemy both in the air and on the ground. One was going to learn to survive the hard way. This was the attitude I had previously experienced at the OTU at Ismailia but I realised now it was a nursery compared to this.

My honest opinion was that somebody had made a big mistake somewhere and I should not be here. The mysterious machine-cum-human complex called RAF Records Office – always a source of cynical amusement to all members of the RAF – had boobed somewhere along the line. Of that I was sure.

VIII

The Big Push

The squadron, as previously mentioned, formed No 125 Wing with 41 and 350 (Belgian) Squadrons, all flying Spitfire Mark XIVs, under the command of Group Captain Scott-Malden. The wing was in No 83 Group commandered by Air Vice-Marshal Harry Broadhurst and formed part of the 2nd Tactical Air Force in support of the Canadian and British 21st Army Group, under the command of General Montgomery. Until the middle of March the three squadrons had been operating as individual units from different bases. 130 was the leading squadron of the wing and the only one based at Eindhoven. As the army advanced towards the Rhine, the distances from Eindhoven to the targets and back were extending, shortening the patrols over the area. During this time from 9 February, I learnt they had taken a severe beating resulting in the shortage of pilots. This explained the numerous questions and the perplexing state of morale when the bold, but innocent Musketeer turned up.

Operation Varsity (the crossing of the Rhine) was imminent, and 130 Squadron took part in low-level pre-strikes against fortified positions, cutting transport and communication links, providing cover for the fighter-bombers attacking anti-aircraft batteries amassed on the east bank. One of its most dangerous but successful ground-attacks was to put a large front line Luftwaffe base out of action. Rheine (a large Luftwaffe fighter base) despite being bombed numerous times still operated squadrons of Me109g's, FW190's and Me262 Jets, although 262's were so few they were only seen operating in small sections or as singletons. It was only ten miles from the Dutch border and extremely well defended. The threat to the bridgehead was obvious; they held the balance. 83 Group were ordered to attack and wipe out the Luftwaffe fighters.

In conjunction with other squadrons, 130 ceaselessly attacked the stationary fighters, and those in the act of taking off to engage or escape. The flak was so heavy it menaced their own aircraft. Those

that did get airborne were easy targets for the attackers at climbing
speed. One gaggle (enemy formation) of 30 plus returning to base
were either short of fuel, ammunition, or nerve, and cleared off
without engaging the Spitfires. The Luftwaffe fighters retreated
inland. The operations took their toll of RAF pilots of course, a
number didn't return, entirely due to the extremely heavy flak. The
strike force accomplished what it set out to do. Numerous
unserviceable aircraft including the first Me262's to be captured by
the advancing ground forces were left behind.

When I joined the squadron, this activity was still in progress, I
wasn't included in any of the sorties to Rheine until the last resort,
presumably I had to take someone's place, making up the numbers
and showing a larger force. Apart from a few hairy moments I
remained intact, but didn't contribute much to the action. On
subsequent sorties I took part in over the area all was quiet and apart
from ground attacks on MET (mechanical enemy transports) and
railway stock there was little to record.

Leading up to 24 March, D-Day for crossing the Rhine, 130
Squadron carried out over 70 sorties in two days clearing the area
behind the Rhine of mobile enemy forces before flying continuous
sweeps in depth east of the Rhine to tempt Luftwaffe fighters to come
to combat. These were 'rodeos'. Other tactics called 'circuses' – a
formation of light-bombers heavily defended by fighters – were also
employed to motivate enemy fighters to engage, but none of it had
the desired effect. Field Marshal Galland held them back in
readiness for Montgomery's assault. Operations once again resorted
to ground attacks (armed reconnaissances) shooting at anything
that moved, including horses. The Germans used many horse-drawn
vehicles.

Patrolling up and down the designated crossing areas, one could
see the troops and equipment massing on the west bank of the Rhine,
the British Second Army and Canadian First Army northwards and
the Americans to the south. So we knew the big push was imminent.
It was a fascinating sight watching the Royal Engineers assembling
boats and Bailey bridges in the rear. All the existing bridges had
been destroyed of course, by the retreating Germans.

The big day arrived on 24 March: Operation Varsity. We were
ordered to provide an umbrella over the northern end of the
dropping zone, the British 1st Commando and 6th Airborne
Division with the US 17th Airborne Division established a

bridgehead between Rees and Wesel over the Rhine and for three days thousands of troops and equipment were landed by gliders on the east bank, sustaining heavy casualties from mobile flak units. Ensconced batteries had been taken out by the ground-attack fighters. The strategem was successful because No 1 Commando occupied the landing areas before airborne troops were landed on the east bank. Frankly, I was out of my depth in the milling, hurly-burly of the action. Aircraft were everywhere, above and below us, and it was a problem distinguishing enemy fighter-bombers from other friendly patrols. A wing of Thunderbolt fighters in the wrong sector persisted in bouncing us from above and the boss had his work cut out trying to keep us together and taking avoiding action; this distracted us from our job of giving the RAF fighter-bombers and Typhoons protective cover from enemy fighters. We arrived back without loss.

At Arnhem the brass-hats deemed that fighters and ground-support fighter-bombers wouldn't be needed over the dropping zone, and banned them from the area. They obviously learnt, albeit the hard way, that they owed a tremendous vote of thanks to the Spitfire IX fighter-bombers and rocket-firing Typhoons this time; whilst the fighter screen was too tight for the Luftwaffe fighter-bombers to penetrate it to cause any serious damage to the bridgehead. History records what a shambles Arnhem was.

Other duties entailed escorting light/medium bombers of No 2 Group (Mitchells and Bostons) in their low level attacks on hidden enemy troops in the forest with anti-personnel fragmentation bombs, and high explosives on the Panzer divisions. It was a round the clock operation, as one box of bombers left the target, another one arrived, ceaselessly pounding the massed German armour lying in wait for the Allies after they crossed the river. The flak was so intensive, it kept the Luftwaffe's fighters away, and most of the casualties suffered by the RAF and USAAF were entirely due to the heavy fire of the light A/A German batteries.

As the opposition shrunk in the air – it didn't amount to much anyway – the squadron was split into sections again, strafing and harassing motor transports, tanks and 'train-busting'. Across the river the ground forces met little opposition after three days of heavy bombing on the town of Weser – the key crossing point – forcing the Germans to fall back.

Gradually gaining confidence, I was unfortunate to have radio trouble on two occasions and on the first one, I had no alternative but to return to base after we had attacked a Wehrmacht forward field HQ and control post situated in the small town of Nienburg. The HQ building was in a square at the head of the main street, so we had to fly up the street on the deck in order to make the most impact on the building and to avoid the heavy fire of 37mm-calibre flak surrounding it. Following the boss in line astern, we peeled off from 5,000 ft, diving down through the flak to the end of the street, levelled off between the attics of the straight thoroughfare, to see the facade of the Nazi HQ with all its flags flying dead ahead of us, we couldn't miss. Our 20mm shells blasted into it like cutting cheese, before having to haul the stick back hard to avoid the chimney stacks, and climbing like a bat out of hell over a flak battery in the rear of the building. As the range lengthened I got my breath back and rejoined the boss to discover my transmitter had packed in. I signalled by hand and he indicated to break formation and head for base, Mike sailed up alongside me with orders to escort me home.

The squadron winged away looking for more trouble. Arriving back at base the electrician found that a small piece of shrapnel was responsible for cutting the leads of the transmitter, but I was completely unaware of it. I never felt a thing as they say. The damage inflicted inside the German field headquarters must have been fairly substantial. When we returned later for a further attack on the building, the Nazi flags were gone, the flak batteries were no longer there and no sign of any military activity was apparent; the SS had seemingly evacuated the town.

The second one was more dramatic; on 27 March on an armed reconnaissance in the Munster area where we wiped out a mobile column, we unexpectedly came across a *Staffel* (squadron) of long-nosed FW190's as we climbed back to 10,000 feet, closing at right angles on a collision course at the same altitude. They suddenly appeared out of cumulus cloud, and both formations were taken completely by surprise. I was so close to them I could easily see the black crosses, squadron markings and a pilot looking straight at me. The first impression was their sinister appearance; it was my first encounter with enemy fighters at close range. Unfortunately they were *too* close, barely one hundred yards away and there wasn't even time to take the safety catch off the trigger. 'Finger trouble' was the RAF term for it – asleep, in other words.

At that precise moment we swept into another cloud, I saw our flight leader (Flight Lieutenant Walmsley) turn into a steep climb which would put him on a parallel course with the Germans and I stuck to him like glue until he disappeared completely in cloud. I heard him shout 'Tally ho' on the radio but I was completely blinded and continued the climb and turn with the throttle lever 'through the gate' (buster) giving maximum emergency speed. When I emerged from the cloud having gained another 5,000 feet, all I could see was dots on the horizon going in all directions, scattered to the winds. It was impossible to identify any of the aircraft and the radio was silent. Calling Red Leader brought no response. The dots had all disappeared and I was entirely alone.

I realised I had made my first tactical blunder by opening up to full throttle. I should have reduced speed to make a much tighter bank and turn, which would have kept me in contact with the leader at such close quarters. But suddenly blinded by cloud, I had no idea where he had gone and the recognized tactic was to buster whenever one went into action. This was what I was taught back at school. Maximum power was paramount. However, we live and learn as they say.

Circling around, hoping someone would show up, I heard faint voices in the headphones but indistinguishable. I set a rough course for base, having no idea where I was except that I was deep in enemy territory. Receiving no replies to my calls to Red Leader and our sector controller, I realised that my transmitter was either dead or I was out of range.

Normally in these circumstances operating in the UK radar would pick up one's transmission and send a course to steer to return to base, but after trying all the frequencies available including the emergency channel, I gave it up. Eventually picking up a landmark on the map, a mathematical calculation gave me a dead-reckoning course to steer home. I was deeper into Germany than I thought, and more calculations ascertained that I had little fuel to play with. Steering home at a bare cruising speed like a cat on hot bricks, craning my neck around, hoping no Luftwaffe fighter spotted me, I heard a loud excited voice over the airwaves, shouting, 'Tally ho'.

Banking round I saw a large formation tearing towards me from behind. I recognized them as Spitfires and the voices as Canadians. I pressed my radio button and transmitted my call-sign but to no avail; the transmitter was dead. This bunch bore down on me like hornets, and excited chatter filled the headphones. I could not understand it; if I could recognize them as Spitfires, why on earth couldn't these trigger-happy morons recognize me? The fundamental fighter tactic was always to turn head-on into the attacker but would these twits recognize a Spitfire coming at them head-on? I rather doubted it. The general public those days would be surprised to learn of some of the most stupid mistakes that were made, and not in the heat of the battle either.

I had two choices. Firstly, I could open up and leave them standing. I had so much greater power than they could command. I knew they could only be flying the Mark IX which was the common and most numerous of Spitfires equipped by squadrons on the second front. They were not in the same class as the one I was flying although they were a very efficient fighter. However, I was very short of fuel, and couldn't afford to show them a clean pair of heels over a long distance and they might have just taken off with full tanks. I would dearly have loved to demonstrate the superior speed this aircraft had over theirs, and given them the surprise of their lives.

The only other course open to me was to identify myself to these idiots – I didn't suffer fools gladly. I banked steeply towards them displaying the unmistakable outline of the Spitfire mainplanes to them until I had one of them in my sights, as the range decreased to 200 yards. I could have shot him down but skimming over the top of him I banked back to my original course, to see the formation was in disarray all around me.

The penny dropped at last, I heard howls of disappointment. 'J . . . . . it's one of ours. Bloody hells bells, just our bloody luck, damn him.' Charming sentiments, were they not? Typically profound colonial language. Nobody broke off to have a friendly look at me to check if I was OK; oh, no, they just cleared off – I must have shamed them – leaving a very relieved pilot still in one piece. Believe it or not, this was the fate of many lone pilots recorded, but mostly unrecorded. Getting back on course I navigated back to Eindhoven to find the rest of the section of eight had landed.

A carnival air greeted me, I thought it because of my safe return, but no such thing: the morale of the squadron was sky-high, celebrations were in order. I made my report. The leader thought I had bought it when communications went dead, but the boss was happy to report no losses in his report to Group. Everyone was so preoccupied with the victories, I didn't think it worth mentioning the little nerve-racking incident with the Canadian squadron. The irony of it was that Sergeant Georgie Warren scored on his first trip. Lucky blighter, I thought.

A report filtered through the channels from the ground crew to the effect that when they came to refuelling my aircraft, there were only three gallons of fuel in the tanks. One of them said to me later when I went to see what the trouble with the radio transmitter was, 'You cut it a bit fine, didn't you, Sarge? We thought the bowser meter was faulty.' Of course, all fuel, ammunition etc. was recorded on the aeroplane's maintenance form; it was necessary to find out the cause of the excessive fuel used in comparison with the other aircraft on that flight, to check there was no fault. In my search for the section after the encounter with the Focke Wulfs and then searching for a landmark to pin-point my position, I had obviously been going round in circles. The fuel gauge in the cockpit was found to be incorrectly calibrated, consequently I was unaware that I had less fuel than indicated. It was sheer luck that ended it happily for me. Fortunately or unfortunately whichever way one looked at it, another fault prevented the fuel pressure warning light illuminating to warn me I was not going to make it and I might have baled out to be on the safe side before reaching base. On the other hand, the engine may have cut on the approach to the runway, so although I hadn't suffered any damage I literally came in on a wing and a prayer, and didn't know! The gods were with me, without doubt: three times in that one trip, I could have bought it. Yet at other times, other chaps only had the one chance, and lost.

The CO mentioned it the next day, jokingly asking me if I had been on a one-man sortie after getting lost. I told him in an equally light-hearted vein, 'A whole bloody squadron chased me, but they weren't bloody Huns.' He was in a very happy frame of mind after the squadron's success the previous day, and he laughed and said, 'You'll do, lad, I was surprised you turned up at all.' An ambiguous remark if ever there was one. Then he said sternly that I should have reported it for everyone's benefit; the electrician found a fault in the wiring when he replaced the radio which might not have come to light. Consequently the next pilot to use that particular Spitfire may have come to grief through no fault of his own. Another lesson to be learnt.

Phil Clay was credited with two kills to bring his score to four. Mike Ockendon was unlucky; he had one in his sights when he himself was attacked from the rear and he had to break off the

Year 1945 Month	Date	AIRCRAFT Type	No.	Pilot, or 1st Pilot	2nd Pilot, Pupil or Passenger	DUTY (Including Results and Remarks)
—	..	—		—	—	—— Totals Brought Forward
APRIL	4	SPITFIRE XIV	AP-Z	SELF	—÷—	ARMED RECCE (LINGEN AREA)
"	4	SPITFIRE XIV	AP-Z	SELF	—÷—	ARMED RECCE (LINGEN AREA)
"	5	SPITFIRE XIV	AP-N	SELF	—÷—	ARMED RECCE (LINGEN AREA)
"	7	SPITFIRE XIV	AP-H	SELF	—÷—	EINDHOVEN - TWENTE - EINDHOVEN
"	7	SPITFIRE XIV	AP-H	SELF	—÷—	EINDHOVEN - TWENTE (NEW BASE)
"	8	SPITFIRE XIV	AP-N	SELF	—÷—	BRIDGEHEAD PATROL (NIENBURG)
"	9	SPITFIRE XIV	AP-H	SELF	—÷—	PATROL (DÜMMER LAKE - QUAKENBRÜ)
"	9	SPITFIRE XIV	AP-V	SELF	—÷—	PATROL (" " ")
"	10	SPITFIRE XIV	AP-V	SELF	—÷—	PATROL (LINGEN AREA)
"	10	SPITFIRE XIV	AP-V	SELF	—÷—	PATROL (" ")
"	11	SPITFIRE XIV	AP-Z	SELF	—÷—	PATROL (BREMEN - VERDEN)
"	12	SPITFIRE XIV	AP-A	SELF	—÷—	PATROL (BREMEN - NIENBURG)
"	12	SPITFIRE XIV	AP-D	SELF	—÷—	PATROL (" ")
"	13	SPITFIRE XIV	AP-J	SELF	—÷—	PATROL (BREMEN AREA)
"	13	SPITFIRE XIV	AP-J	SELF	—÷—	PATROL (" ")
"	14	SPITFIRE XIV	RN 691	SELF	—÷—	EINDHOVEN - TWENTE
"	16	SPITFIRE XIV	AP-Y	SELF	—÷—	PATROL (BREMEN - RETHEM)
"	16	SPITFIRE XIV	AP-D	SELF	—÷—	TWENTE - CELLE (NEW BASE)
"	17	SPITFIRE XIV	AP-N	SELF	—÷—	ARMED RECCE (SCHWERM AREA)
"	17	SPITFIRE XIV	AP-J	SELF	—÷—	ARMED RECCE
"	18	SPITFIRE XIV	AP-Z	SELF	—÷—	ARMED RECCE
"	20	SPITFIRE XIV	AP-A	SELF	—÷—	ARMED RECCE (LUBECK AREA)

GRAND TOTAL [Cols. (1) to (10)]
.................Hrs. ....Mins.

Totals Carried Forward

SINGLE-ENGINE AIRCRAFT				MULTI-ENGINE AIRCRAFT						PASS-ENGER	INSTR/CLOUD FLYING [incl. in cols. (1) to (10)]	
DAY		NIGHT		DAY			NIGHT					
Dual	Pilot	Dual	Pilot	Dual	1st Pilot	2nd Pilot	Dual	1st Pilot	2nd Pilot		Dual	Pilot
(1)	(2)	(3)	(4)	(5)	(6)	(7)	(8)	(9)	(10)	(11)	(12)	(13)
0·15	176·50	12·00	5·00								27·15	
	1·10	R/T failed in electrical storm, grim weather.										
	1·00	Section returned, visibility too poor.										
	1·30	12 MET in flames. Flak heavy.										
	1·00	CLAIMED 1st Kill on recce over TWENTE. FW 190 seen dropping in flames.										
	1·15	KILL CONFIRMED AT ENSCHEDE. ME 109G damaged at NIJMEGEN.										
	1·25	Nothing but flak was our lot. ME 262 in abundance but too fast.										
	·50	No Huns seen. Hit by flak in engine, returned base. Proved to be AMERICAN FLAK later.										
	1·30	Bounced by gaggle of 30 odd FW TA 152's - lost 2 of section of 4.										
	·10	A/C o/s. Returned base.										
	1·35	No Huns seen.										
	1·25	Uneventful except S/Ldr Hume destroyed JU 88 at Stade airfield										
	1·30	Ammo train completely destroyed - F/Lt Sillett hit by debris										
	1·50	Convoy 12 MET. - 4 destroyed 7 damaged.										
	1·50	No Huns seen										
	1·45	,, ,,										
	·30	Delivery flight.										
	1·55	Damaged JU 188 over NIENBURG - Probable - Glycol streaming out of port engine.										
	·40	SQDN move to new base										
	1·00	Damaged 1 LOCO - 1 TRUCK - 1 ARMOURED CAR										
	·35	u/c u/s returned base, hit by flak.										
	1·25	Damaged 2 TRUCKS, 3 half-tracks + 1 tank										
	1·20	Ran into 8 FW 190's, section of 4 scored 2 destroyed (- F/Lt Wilmsley, + Consford)										
		1 damaged. (2/Lt Consford) - Tail-plane shot up.										
	27·00											
0·15	176·50	12·00	5·00				✓				27·15	
	203·50											
(1)	(2)	(3)	(4)	(5)	(6)	(7)	(8)	(9)	(10)	(11)	(12)	(13)

A page from the author's log-book, 4–20 April 1945.

engagement to save himself. He did Flight Lieutenant Sibeth a good turn by attracting the Focke-Wulf inadvertently, making the German a sitting target for Sibeth to shoot down. The section on the inside turn of the squadron were the ones with most success, they had a clear view in an ideal position when the *Staffel* crossed ahead of them, with no cloud to hinder them. It was merely a question of chasing and hitting them from behind with superior speed, the Germans only wished to escape.

On that memorable day, our wing commander, Group Captain David Scott-Malden, said goodbye and relinquished command of 125 Wing to the famed newly promoted Group Captain (Johnnie) J.E. Johnson, DSO, DFC. The weather turned sour and for the following fortnight the squadron flew only in sections of four on patrol. The boss was away at briefings and conferences at Brussels. The Luftwaffe fighters were conspicuous by their absence, so it was a waste of manpower and fuel to operate more than four Spitfires in a sortie. The Luftwaffe fighters were averse to flying when the weather was poor, which wasn't lost on our commanders, who interpreted it as a shortage of leaders. For us it meant more flights but fewer pilots. I was regularly flying in sections of four now, generally as wingman to the section leaders. In sections of four and six we constantly patrolled various sectors on reconnaissance along the front line, looking for enemy activity both in the air and on the ground, but with little success in finding it.

April started off with very poor weather, but nevertheless in the absence of the Luftwaffe, the sections hammered the mobile enemy columns. I was getting plenty of practice in now, I lost count of the number of armed METs and mobile Flakbatterie we annihilated. On one sortie, Flying Officer Finbow was unlucky. I saw him hit by flak as he passed over the last vehicle, but fortunately he crash-landed inside our lines and quickly sent to hospital.

In one period after that, it was exciting work not knowing what to expect when there were only four of us winging along, but little did happen for a while. Then on our second trip one day in the late evening, we sighted a huge gaggle of mixed enemy fighters Messerschmitt BF 109g's and FW190s heading south-east. They were flying very high, towards us at one o'clock. Our altitude was 5,000 feet, there was little point in flying higher for we couldn't see any activity on the ground at a greater height. The light was fading fast and even at that height little could be seen on the ground; the weak sun however lit up the enemy above in a clear sky. They couldn't see us against the back-cloth of the dark ground and our leader called up control and made his report. We had no orders to engage a superior force of such strength and I thought we would put our noses down and get to hell out of it, but the leader ordered us to climb right. We closed in on him to tighten the formation as he gradually increased the rate of turn and climb. For the life of me I couldn't guess where his tactics were going to lead us. He suddenly screamed, 'Buster Red section.' Pushing the throttle lever through the safety gate for maximum power and steepening the climb until we were practically hanging on our props underneath the leading *Staffel* of the cruising enemy force, we clawed our way upwards. It must have been a whole *Jagdgruppe* – a wing of roughly 30/40 fighters in RAF terms – flying in a steppped-up line-astern formation, probably moving to a new base inland.

Fully expecting them to spot us any second, I was in a cold sweat. I didn't know what the twit leading us was going to do next. We could not get above them, an impossibility. They didn't see us luckily – intent on reaching their airfield before darkness forced the use of a flare-path to get down – we were 3,000 feet below the main body when the leader bellowed out, 'OK, chaps, get stuck in.' I couldn't believe my ears: attacking a force of fighters at half their speed, from *below*, and hopelessly outnumbered? Ludicrous, I thought it would have been a better idea to follow them at a low height, and hopefully return with intelligence of the direction and area of their destination. A full scale attack on them could have been mounted by fighter-bombers in the morning, whilst they were on the ground. The range and fading light might have defeated us, but it was worth trying.

There was so much interference on the radio, I could hardly make out a word. We were no longer in formation – with throttles through the gate at emergency power, some engines had more power than others of course, depending on the wear and tear. I heard somebody gabble, 'Bloody engine's knackered.' Out of the corner of my eye I saw a Spit stall and flick over onto his back into a spin, I watched him recover but that was the last I saw of him in the gloom. We were climbing at 3,800 ft per minute at 190 mph, the engine and superchargers were deafening in their protest. A long four minutes had elapsed from the first sighting, as the shadows above took shape, passed over us and disappeared, leaving our section dispersed in the gloom fighting for height. The stepped-up tail of the gaggle passed five hundred feet above me without seeing me, and vanished at a rate of knots with the last rays of the winter sun behind them, there was no chance of catching a straggler; the time limit at maximum boost was already surpassed.

I stooged around for a while and decided to make for base before it was too dark to find it and I didn't want to encourage our own A/A gunners to have a go at me by mistake. I could see some flashes of tracer in the distance where the enemy aircraft had passed but everything was obscure. Flying over a darkened countryside was a new experience but it was a clear evening and I had no trouble finding the airfield.

Once again I landed alone and taxied back to the dispersal to be greeted with some concern at the operations hut, nobody except me had come back so far, and no-one knew what had happened. A scrambled Tempest squadron returned, reporting they had seen nothing. Feeling damn tired and sick, I told the spies all I knew of the action, of the other three I knew nothing. Inwardly I was adamant that if he survived I would never fly with that particular leader again. Time went by and there was no news of the rest of the section. The deputy CO, one of the flight commanders, was engulfed in anxiety. It was a freelance reconnaissance, and he would ultimately be responsible for the consequences. My report could only be taken at face value until it was corroborated and that put me in a very awkward position. I couldn't blow the gaff. No enemy aircraft were shot down.

One officer was missing, another flying officer recently transferred to our squadron was believed to have been shot down over enemy territory – an army outpost had seen a Spitfire in flames and no other Allied aircraft were known to be airborne at the time. The leader was posted as missing, so I was the only known survivor. However he breezed in the next day, as though nothing had happened. Engine failure, he said.

My first real clanger with the squadron occurred a short while before this traumatic incident and requires a short explanation.

The Spitfire XIV RR Griffon engine was started with a Coffman cartridge, an entirely different system from the way the Merlin engine was started. The premise of its advantage was that it did not require any ground crew to assist in starting, cutting manpower, especially on an emergency strip, or an airfield only equipped for other types of aircraft.

The Merlin was started by an electrical motor in the engine which derived its power from a battery either in the aircraft or from a powerful mobile two-wheeled trailer linked up to it. The Coffman starter was non-electrical and was similar to a very large bore gun minus the barrel with a magazine of six cartridges. It was a very awkward, precise system no one liked. The engine was primed and a cartridge inserted in the breech block by means of a toggle in the cockpit. One pressed the starter button which in actual fact triggered the hammer and fired the cartridge, similar to a gun. The explosive discharge entered the cylinders and turned the engine with some force and the sparking plugs fired the mixture of fuel and air, thus starting the engine. It had to be primed exactly: if it was too weak, or over-rich which was worse, it failed to bring the engine to life. If it didn't start, one adjusted the priming and selected another cartridge, fired it and hoped for the best.

On this occasion the squadron were to be led by our new wing commander, Group Captain Johnnie Johnson, at full strength on a sortie over Germany. I was allocated his wingman (No 2). My aircraft was the furthest away from the Flight hut. In retrospect, it always was! No pressure was on the leader to start up but everyone else was like a cat on hot bricks waiting for him and his signal to taxi out to the runway. Once on the taxi track it was impossible to overtake any aircraft in front and it was tricky manoeuvring into position on the end of the runway if one was one of the last to reach it, especially if one's position was with the leader! It was always a mad scramble to get into line in one's proper position as the squadron taxied out from the dispersal. Since the heavy surprise attack on New Year's Day, on all the Second Tactical Air Force bases in the Low Countries; during which Eindhoven sustained heavy losses of aircraft on the ground, all aircraft were dispersed well away from each other. Prior to that incident, airfield defences had been reduced and camouflage netting was sent back to the UK by AOC Coningham. Consequently the airfield defences reverted back to the old system with the addition of hurriedly constructed anti-blast walls that shut out one's view of the hut and the leaders. One had to rely on an erk standing within sight of the leader to signal when he started his engine. The offensive role of fighter squadrons no longer required pilots to sit around the dispersal hut at readiness, dressed for instant flight, waiting fot the order to scramble as in the days of the Battle of Britain when their role was purely defensive. Apart from the attack in force on all the airfields by enemy raiders on that New Year's Day there hadn't been any since D-Day. All operational orders came from Group headquarters well in advance, (although the squadron CO could add to them at his discretion) schedules were drawn up, times of take-off chalked up with aircraft allocated to various operations and pilots.

The dispersal point itself was so far away from the runway that many times I've had to taxi like a bat out of hell at 40 mph with an erk hanging on like grim death, in a prone position on each wing-tip and one on the tail-plane for added weight. These chaps took a tremendous risk of falling off as one weaved along taxi tracks in disrepair, trying to avoid holes.

The old clapped-out Spitfire allocated to me, RM 698 AP–Z, wouldn't start at the first attempt. In a panic I pulled the toggle to select another cartridge and pressed the button. She fired like a rocket, smoke and flames belched out of the exhaust with a tremendous roar, I wasn't too happy when sheets of flame flashed through the forward bulkhead invading the cockpit, raising the temperature somewhat and scorching my eyebrows. The hood was still open – never closed until after take-off – and when I was enveloped in thick choking black smoke, I thought it was about time I got to hell out of this; it was like sitting on a time-bomb. I had a nasty feeling that the old girl was about to end her life in a spectacular fashion. It happened so suddenly, merely a flashback I thought, but I misjudged it badly. By their swift action the ground crew didn't.

Flaming fuel streamed from the engine, filling the drip-pan underneath to overflowing. Unstrapping hardness and chute, I heaved myself out of the cockpit and leaped off the mainplane and dived for cover under a tarpaulin. The two ground crew chaps who strapped me in hadn't stayed around to undo their handiwork; they had vanished like the wind and the whole crew had beat a hasty retreat behind a blast wall! Who could blame them? Not me. My thick clothing saved me from a nasty roasting, although the knees were frizzled and scorched, long-johns, the last line of defence kept all the essentials in proper order; we never wore the leather trousers of the Irvin suit. My upper-half where the heat was most intense funnily enough was unscathed, the thick leather flying jacket and helmet saw to that. Apart from a black face, singed eyebrows, and stinking of burnt oil and fuel, I was fine.

She was well alight when to my amazement the intrepid Phil Clay, who wasn't flying on that operation, came dashing along the road with an extinguisher and set about the fire without any concern for his own safety. It was a wasted effort, but to my intense relief that the fuel tanks didn't explode. He could have met his Maker in the most unexpected of places, he admitted later. But it hadn't occurred to him until the oxygen bottle exploded. The fire was soon extinguished by the volunteer fire crew of the squadron; the station crash-tenders were on the other side of the airfield near the runways and it was all over before they reached the dispersal. No one was injured but the aircraft was a write-off.

I didn't know the technical reason for the accident but I had to make a report. I had that uneasy feeling I was going to get a rocket whatever the reason. The ground crew thought it was one big laugh.

'You should have seen your face, Sarge; it was a picture,' they said.

'Thanks a lot,' I replied sarcastically. 'You scarpered off a bit smartly, didn't you? Just like a bunch of bloody rabbits with a ferret after them.' That took the grins off their faces, but there was no animosity between us.

The operation went smoothly, but the boss was irritated when 'Johnnie' Johnson's wingman didn't turn up, unaware of the accident that had kept them waiting on the runway, and subsequently had to rearrange the disposition of the squadron of 11 aircraft. I considered I'd had a lucky escape, so what?

Little was said then and I tried to forget about it on my next trip, I hoped it wasn't going to be a habit! The ground crew exaggerated their movements as soon as I was strapped in after that, by leaping away from the aircraft and keeping a safe distance away from it until the engine started. Of course they were taking the mickey. At the dispersal hut my fellow pilots joined in, chaffing me remorselessly amid ribald hilarity; I was the chap who baled out on the deck; I was the only chap ever to 'shoot himself down'; and a gem of a quote: 'Didn't know you felt the cold so much, old man.' I took it all in good part, getting my revenge on them in horseplay, filling their boots with tin tacks after they'd gone to sleep, and putting smoke pellets I'd wangled out of the armourers underneath their beds when we were at dinner. The administrative types weren't amused; new bedding had to be found, but there was no danger of a fire and once the smell had dissipated everything was back to normal. The score was even.

It was not the end of the matter. A week later I had to report to HQ No 83 Group Eindhoven and hand over my log-book. After waiting awhile an orderly returned it to me and told me I was free to go. It was a mysterious trip until I looked at the back page of my log. In red ink it stated I had disobeyed orders leading to the loss of one Spitfire RM 698; punishment not applicable; signed Group Captain J.E. Johnson. The charge read: '. . . failing to wait one minute before inserting a second cartridge in the breech, thus contravening Air Ministry instructions as laid down in the Pilot's Handbook, applicable to Spitfire Mark XIV; resulting in an excessive charge damaging the combustion chambers leading to the subsequent fire and destruction of the aircraft. . .'

It was a very obscure rule, in fact the handbook referred to was a guide for pilots and not strictly a regulation, so a feverish hunt was on for a tattered, dog-eared, torn handbook on the Spitfire XIV. We eventually found a copy and the relevant passage. You might know: it had never happened to anyone else, certainly pilots had gone through the same procedure as many times as I had, but this was the first time it had caused a fire. The technical clerks must have had eyes like saucers to find the hidden, small type instruction in the book. Of course the fault was in the cartridge or it hadn't been stored in a dry place, therefore it was a million to one chance of a fire if the fuel pipes and carburettor were airtight, which they obviously weren't.

The boss agreed that one couldn't just sit there hoping the engine would start, especially in a scramble; it was absurd. Apart from that, one was unable to keep cool, calm and collected when the shadow of such a distinguished leader as 'Johnnie Johnson' loomed over one like the 'sword of Damocles'. One had to run two hundred yards in full gear, get strapped in and start the engine, check all the instruments etc. and be ready to move off behind him at the same time as he did; but he had no leg work. He laughed, don't take life so seriously, he said. The Groupie was just another pilot. He went on to say, 'Don't attach too much importance to the entry in your log. Someone has to carry the can of losing a £10,000 fighter and you are the candidate.' It was convenient that way, it saved expensive inquiries, he said. It could not be proved unless someone stood there with a stop-watch. 'Take my advice, old lad. Just forget it. If you get through the war with no further trouble, you'll be bloody lucky.' His nonchalant, lack of interest in the episode was surprising; I was still under the influence of the rigid discipline of the training schools. He wasn't disturbed in the least, but during training it would have been a cardinal sin and the end of one's career. Oh for the old electrical starter battery that was used to start the Merlin engines, so simple and positive.

The incident had its compensation: it gave me the satisfaction that I was needed. The boss had a ready-made excuse to get rid of me, and the wing commander wasn't interested in censuring or reprimanding me personally, and they had just gone through the mandatory motions. If my feelings seem odd to the reader, I should explain that this was a different Air Force to the one I knew during training. I felt insecure on the squadron. Instructor officers spent a great deal of time with one, even if one didn't like what they had to say, they were helpful. Here, a malaise overhung everybody and no one ever had a word of advice to offer; on the other hand, no one had any criticism to make. A rocket from someone or a pat on the back would have been welcomed, but apart from the boss, I had no real identity or affinity with my flight commander or anyone. One hoped that one was doing the right thing, and it wasn't until something untoward happened as in this case that one knew where one stood. I was rapidly coming to the conclusion that I was too tense, too keyed up and too eager, but it was inherent and there was little I could do; a leopard cannot change his spots.

So far, I was obviously up to the standard in the role allocated to me in the squadron; considered by my superiors to be able to play my part with a promising future, but I didn't feel this potential was being exploited to the full, through lack of combat training.

On the other hand, one has either got what it takes or not. Mock battles within the squadron would have helped me tremendously, but there was no time for such frivolities. Flying in a section of four or whatever the number, I was Red Two, just another pilot, I had no identity. I wasn't at all happy to be someone's wingman forever, I wanted the opportunity to lead too. Unless I was given that opportunity, I could not see how I could make an impression on my seniors to justify the foretold promising future. I was certainly too reticent to mention it to anyone in case I became the laughing stock of the squadron. Matters would have been extremely happier if all the members of a section flew together in every sortie they were

engaged in, banded together as a team, each one would know the
other three intimately and learn each other's moves; not to mention
the bonhomie between us. Apart from one or two cliques who went
on freelance trips – I was never asked to join them – one flew with
different chaps on every flight, unless it was at squadron strength.
However an individualist such as myself had to bury his own ideas
and put his utmost effort into the job he was required to do, without
reservation. How I longed for one bosom pal in this outfit, someone
that I could talk to and get my feelings off my chest. Someone to have
an affinity with. I had no real friends here. I was anything but a
happy man at this stage.

More and more as time went by I wished I hadn't been so timid in
approaching the boss and asking for a transfer to a photo-
reconnaissance squadron. It may sound egocentric coming from a
mere sergeant. The individual pilots in these units came back from
their lone operations with valuable information. They must have
derived immense satisfaction from a hazardous flight to present a
report to their superiors that had some significance, whatever it may
be. In order to do that he had to contend with poor weather and
attacks from high flying enemy fighters, but he was his own master
and only his individual skills could bring him home.

Fresh tactics sent 83 Group fighters and fighter-bombers deeper
inland whilst 84 Group gave support in the immediate vicinity to the
British Second Army and also diverted north and eastwards in
support of the Canadian First Army heading towards Denmark. No.
130 in 83 Group consequently now ranged further afield into
Germany on sweeps and armed recces to Enschede, Twente (a
Luftwaffe base), Koesfeld, Munster, Bremen, Lingen areas, and
escorting Mitchell medium-bombers to the Borken area.

In early April I did not fly much because of the poor weather.
Warrant Officer Andy Miller was downed on one sweep behind
enemy lines, but managed to escape and make his way back. The
next day despite the weather I flew two sweeps in the Lingen area. In
the first one of nine aircraft we found the target area covered with
10/10th cloud down to 500 feet and my receiver packed in. However,
I told the leader, he put his thumb up indicating he had heard me
and I stuck to him throughout the sweep. I had little choice, I didn't
know our position and there was no way I could break off and
navigate myself back to base under the prevailing conditions. It was
a long one-hour ten-minutes for no reward. The second one in a

section of four was more fruitful, we found a column and destroyed five transports and damaged ten, plus a Tiger tank!

On another of our reconnaissance sweeps, we attacked a heavily defended German ammunition convoy threading its way west, destroying 10 and damaging about 14 vehicles, when Flying Officer Treverrow's enthusiasm carried him away, hitting a tree on pulling out of his dive and damaging his port wing. Fortunately he was able to gain sufficient height to bale out and luck was still with him when he landed on our side of the lines. He hitched his way back to the squadron unscathed, much to our delight.

Montgomery, by-passing the Ruhr, with the British Second Army was moving fast spreading north-eastwards, leaving the First Canadian Army to capture northern Holland and mop up enemy units left behind by the British leaving a few enemy pockets in their haste to catch up with the spearhead. The Luftwaffe left the Wehrmacht in the coastal regions of north-west Holland with no armoured divisions or air cover. The British Second Army with the air support of 83 Group fighter-bombers swept through the north-eastern sector.

They reached Enschede, the last Dutch town by 5 April, turning east towards Hamburg. Our endurance range was now stretched to the limit as the 21st Army Group made rapid progress. The weather was foul but improving. The squadron had to move up to be more effective and spend more time over the operational areas. The weather was holding us back but AVM Broadhurst was in a hurry to press on and 130 received orders to move to Twente airfield, Enschede just inside the border with Germany, immediately it was overrun by the troops. On inspection some of the squadron officers weren't too happy about the state of it. The airfield was waterlogged, and full of craters, the runways bombed out of existence and operationally very dicy. The new wing commander thought otherwise, but after some repairs had been effected, the squadron moved from Eindhoven to Twente (over two days) 6/7 April, landing with some difficulty. Spasmodic flak from a few remnants of the German rearguard didn't help and a few broken props and damaged under-carriages resulted, but with no casualties. Nos 41 and 350 Squadrons rejoined 130 again later to complete the wing. A narrow grass strip was hurriedly made serviceable by the Engineers for take-off on the morrow and we were back in business.

On my first flight to reconnoitre Twente I had my first taste of action in the air. Our section surprised six FW 190's circling the airfield after a short visit there, or perhaps they were the last to leave the airfield. I was lucky. The last one was nearest to me and I don't think he saw me; he actually flew into my path. Spontaneously pressing the button I gave him a long burst but he got away without showing any signs of being hit, so I pursued him whilst the rest of the section chased the others. He hugged the ground to prevent me getting another burst in and suddenly a whisper of smoke poured out of his engine as he climbed into a low-lying cloud. I couldn't find him again, but later on the army reported that they had seen an enemy aircraft crash about ten miles east. No others were seen so I presumed it was mine and I claimed it. The rest of the section claimed kills, but this particular one I was sure was mine due to the region in which the wreckage was found. It was an anti-climax, I didn't see him go down and the resulting interrogation didn't impress me one little bit.

The hurried move from Eindhoven to this God-forsaken hole made itself apparent the next day. The army were ready to cross the Weser and moving to Twente brought it within our range without long range fuel tanks.

At the first glimmer of dawn we made our way to our aircraft standing like ghosts in the misty half-light we climbed aboard and prepared for the first sortie of the day. The cloud base was at ground level and we were stood down until it lifted. Towards lunch-time it lifted to 300 feet and our seniors decided to send off the first section of four of which I was one; using the grass strip running along the boundary we took off in pairs through the drizzle, with the second man formating on the leader. We climbed through 10/10ths cloud to 25,000 ft before it grew lighter and we finally broke cloud into bright sunlight. The boss and I circled until the second pair joined us and formed up into battle formation. The boss set course for the Nienburg bridgehead, over the river Weser 105 miles due east, where the British Second Army had met the next and last obstacle before the Elbe. We arrived in clear skies to see the troops pouring across.

Moving up river to Verden we met two Messerschmitt Me262 jet fighter-bombers (the *Sturmbird*) streaking for the troop concentrations. Stooging along at a greater height, we quickly peeled off into a steep dive in hot pursuit and were actually gaining on them, opening fire on the tail-ender; when they jettisoned their bomb-load well short of their target and zoomed up in a tremendously steep climb at a rate beyond us. Some Tempests joined in and got in the way. One appeared to be damaged as he disappeared out of sight, a flying officer swore that he saw a black dot leave it, but no chute opened. It was very difficult to substantiate kills in the RAF without evidence, unlike the enemy and some American outfits. It was impossible to engage these jets in a dog-fight; we could outmanoeuvre them but their speed was too great. Beyond the maker's limits the Spitfire XIV's aileron control was very difficult in a flat-out dive of well over 500 mph. It never ceased to amaze me the amount of punishment these Spits could take beyond the maker's recommendations, despite the aircraft's objections. The 262s had to be surprised in the first attack otherwise the opportunity was lost. They never engaged Allied fighters, it was pointless.

The jets were incapacitated with bomb-loads – they reduced their maximum speed by 120 mph – which put them in our bracket and vulnerable to attack, but as pure fighters the Me262s (262A–1) would have been a real threat. One of the biggest boobs of the war that Hitler was personally responsible for, was that he insisted on the production of the bomber version taking precedence over the fighter, against the advice of his chief-of fighters, Adolf Galland. In fact the fighter was phased out completely until the very last month of the war, when the demoted Galland led his own wing of them against the Americans B17s (Fortresses) in the last raids over Berlin with tremendous success, shooting down 38 in one individual raid. There was no doubt that these aircraft built in substantial numbers and used as fighters against large bomber formations – much earlier in the campaign – would have held up the end of the war until much later.

On our return the weather had cleared and much to everyone's relief we landed without difficulty. Apart from that little excitement the rest of the patrol was without incidence. The squadron maintained standing patrols in sections over the bridgehead all day, until dark but there was little to report of enemy action. However, the last sortie ended sadly.

Sergeant George Warren had disappeared over the enemy lines whilst strafing enemy road transports at Verden. His section found him; he had crashed but there was no sign of him. It wasn't known if his engine had failed or if he was hit by flak. He was posted as missing. George and I had never flown together since that flight test when we both joined the squadron, less than a month ago, except for that memorable day he destroyed the long-nosed FW190 and I got lost. But that short month seemed an eternity to me; it gave me something to think about and didn't do anything for my morale. I liked George. He was a very quite unassuming type of lad, probably overawed finding himself in a theatre of war, so early in his career, as I had done, but he got on with it. I never heard him complain.

Local labour and prisoners had made some huts livable, we had beds but no mattresses. We found a hut containing bedding on the outskirts and helped ourselves to blankets and palliasses, a farmer was reluctant to part with straw but we persuaded him by bribes and threats to fill our palliasses. The kitchen staff had arrived and a field kitchen was set up, so we got our first hot meal of bacon and eggs, never did a meal taste so delicious. We settled down to make the best of it, supplies were coming in but we weren't happy until the first load of alcoholic beverages and cigarettes arrived. The Advanced Airfield Royal Engineers worked like beavers repairing the installations and soon made the runways serviceable, but we were not to stay long before our next move.

Needless to say, personal hygiene was a problem now. We slept fully clothed; there was no hot water except at the field kitchens and the laundry was a problem. Our clothing began to suffer until we bribed an erk to do our shirts and under-clothing; he got a pot boiling somewhere and began making a business of dhobying. No ironing but at least it was washed in a fashion and smelt of carbolic. Some of it was discarded, but we had some warm high-neck sweaters that were originally white. Dirt, oil, grease and fuel soon made our uniforms scruffy, but nobody cared about little things like that. We kept one uniform tidy for emergencies, in case VIPs and brass hats came snooping around.

We all needed something to cheer us up here and that was in short supply. We could get any amount of spirits but most of the beer went to the ground crews. We set up a business deal with them, trading bottle of gin and rum for crates of brown ale. Whisky was too precious to trade unless it was with the officers but they wouldn't part with beer. The locally brewed lager was palatable but had no alcoholic strength. Consequently there was no demand for it, except as a table drink.

On the boss's last trip on 9 April before his return to UK he bagged a Ju188 coming in to land at Stade airfield, I was behind him and had a poop at it too but there was no doubt it was his victory. He could have left it to others, the flak may have made it his very last flight. There was little action for the rest of the squadron. Personally I was very sorry to see him go, but his operational tour was now expired and he was sent home to New Zealand. He was a great guy, charismatic to the last.

Two days later newly promoted Squadron Leader Frank Woolley DFC, from 350 (Belgian) Squadron – one of our wing – took command officially. He was with us as a flight lieutenant when I arrived and gradually took over. He learnt his profession the hard way with No 602 Squadron, famed for being the first squadron to shoot down an enemy bomber over Britain on the commencement of war, in September 1939 at the mouth of the Firth of Forth during an attack on warships based at Rosyth. Frank Woolley had flown in the distinguished company of Paddy Finucane, Pierre Clostermann, and Al Deere, to mention a few of the fighter aces of the war, becoming a flight leader until he left 602 fighting over the Pas de Calais in August to join 350 and commence operations against the new German weapon – the V2 rocket – in company with 130 who were also engaged. He was another born leader, a brilliant tactician and just as unassuming as our old CO. These chaps were the salt of the earth, getting on with the job without worrying where their next gong was coming from. Phil was promoted from flight sergeant to warrant officer.

The weather improved at Twente and over the next week, the squadron swept over Dummer Lake, Quakenbruck, Lingen, Bremen, Verden, Nienburg and Rethem areas twice a day. Some of them required long range reserve slipper-tanks fitted under the fuselage; it was obvious that the Luftwaffe had fallen back to bases in the rear and we would get little joy until we moved forward again. These under-slung slipper tanks were a flipping nuisance, speed had to be considerably reduced to detach them, when one was most vulnerable: at a fast speed they clung to the underside of the fuselage with the force of the airstream. I was attacked once with it still attached, limiting manoeuvrability, but fortunately the pilot of the Me109 was as baffled as I was, as the aircraft swayed about like a pregnant whale, so he broke it off and I managed to get rid of it. On one of these sorties to Nienburg (11 April) our section of six found the rail marshalling yard. The action was extremely successful, numerous trains were hit including an ammunition train.

Flight Lieutenant Sibley, the leader, was hit by flying debris from it at 500 feet, it was such a terrific explosion, but he gained sufficient height to reach our lines and baled out. He returned later. Of the three locomotives blown up, one was down to me. Sibley was a fine man and a good leader, I didn't know it then but after surviving the war, he was to die on the very last flight before we left Norway nearly eighteen months later.

We had no transport available except for officers, which put us out of reach of the Dutch town of Enschede, there was absolutely nothing to do when not flying but try to sleep on stinking damp beds, fully clothed. We went for walks over the Dutch-German border, to fill the time in, as a group. It was essential to go armed. The revolvers never left our sides at any time for snipers and bands of German troops, cut off from their rearguard, roamed about and lived in the dense woods. Our sidearms were issued as a protection against hostile German civilians, particularly farmers if and when we were shot down in their country. More than one pilot after surviving a crash-landing had been hacked to death at the hands of farm labourers. The RAF tactics were to hold them off until taken prisoner by the police or one of the German armed forces controlling the area, subsequently surrendering to them. Even so reports filtered through disclosing the difficulty guards had to keep the civilians at bay after the surrender.

Without the guns, our little jaunts in the countryside would have invited more trouble than we could have coped with. It was most reassuring to have them dangling on one's thigh for all to see in some villages we came across. In one village fifty or more young men suddenly appeared, lining one side of the village road as we walked along on the opposite side, glancing in the windows of the few shops. One could feel the tension rising as we progressed. I felt my hair beginning to stand on end, not a sound was uttered by them as they stood there in dumb hostility watching our every move. We for our part ignored them but quietly kept watchful and alert for any sinister move by them. Phil had his usual aggressive look about him, his hand was resting on the butt of his revolver in its holster, but hoping the need didn't arise to give him an excuse to use it – the rest of our five-man band laughed and joked our way along the street, which seemed to puzzle the onlookers. The silence was oppressive, one little spark and we felt we would be in a pitched battle although as far as we could see, they had no arms. We couldn't turn back and give them the satisfaction that we were frightened of the mob nor had we any intention of integrating with them, so after walking the full length of the village and examining a memorial and water fountain we sauntered back the way we had come. There was no doubt in our minds, that if we had been unarmed we would have been torn to pieces.

Surreptitious glances told us that they were all males between the ages of 16 and 25. The incident was very strange indeed, I was under the impression that all German manpower was in the German armed forces. To find such a large number in such a small village was an enigma. The only other possible explanation was that they were Dutch and either didn't recognize us as British, or they were hostile to us. For most of the war the majority of the Dutch supported the Germans; they were Germanic and actually had tens of thousands of members of the NSP (the Dutch Nazi Party) fighting for the Germans against the Russians! But that is another story. On the border they were all pretty well integrated through marriage, and of course the amount of damage inflicted by the RAF whatever the nationality, on towns, villages and farms (wherever the enemy may be) didn't make Allied airmen very popular with the locals.

One day, one of the most unexpected, but tremendously happy moments of my operational life was about to enfold as we made our way back through the woods to the airfield. A Bedford truck belting along the road stopped ahead of us and a chap in the passenger seat shouted back. 'Climb aboard if you want a lift.' As the boys were clambering over the tail-board, it struck me there was something familiar about that voice. It had a Scottish accent for one thing. Going forward to the cab to investigate, this head came out of the open window and said, 'Get a bloody move on, or get a bloody taxi, I haven't got all flipping day.' A taxi! The apparition staring down was, of all the people in the world, none other than Johnny Dick. He jumped down and unashamedly we hugged each other with howls of joy, to the amusement of the driver and my mates. He was in full flying gear, he had been shot down but escaped with minor injuries in one of the actions we ourselves had been engaged in the day before. Luckily he gained sufficient height to bale out and landed on our side of the line, where he was picked up by the Army and sent on his way, back to his squadron. I couldn't allow that for a little while of course. I diverted the driver to our airfield making him comfortable in our hut and sent up distress signals for food and drink for him and his driver. There was no more flying for us that day so we had 14 hours to spare before the dawn patrol.

In no time at all we had stock of bartered drinks from the airmen's mess tent and set about depleting them as Johnny swapped yarns with us. He hadn't changed a bit; he was his old ebullient self. For the first time Mike and the others were aware of my nickname 'Ashy' when Johnny let the cat out of the bag, I could have throttled him. Anecdotes flowed from him – I think he was still suffering from the shock of his escape. From then on the name stuck with me on the squadron. Our past adventures were an eye-opener for my squadron mates; they must have had a dull past. Johnny kindled the spark, to light up a more friendly, intimate atmosphere. Johnny had a wonderful personality. He was a great raconteur, and had a knack of keeping his listeners' attention. We all needed his intervention to break the ice, from then on I found the going between me and the other NCOs much easier; they had more respect for me. The indefinable suspicious attitude amongst us disappeared. Typhoon pilots were greatly respected; we had seen some of their work against heavily defended areas, literally looking down the barrels of the German guns. About his own operations with Typhoons he had very little to say, but that was quite like the man; he was never one to 'shoot a line'. I thought he looked very tired, certainly he looked older, but his spirit hadn't altered one little bit.

Both of us together in 130 Squadron would have rung the changes, we certainly would have enlivened the mess with our extrovert characteristics. About midnight Phil jumped up and said, 'Let's pep the place up a bit. Follow me, chaps.'

We followed him like sheep by the light of the stars to a hollow at the far side of the airfield. On our arrival we had discovered the Luftwaffe pyrotechnic hut on our exploratory jaunts, full of explosives, rockets and Very light cartridges. The bold Micky broke the door down and we all staggered out with loads of them plus three Very pistols. Some of the objects were as big as a football and we had no idea what they were for. We laid them all out on the meadow and lit the fuses. They went off with a tremendous bang and soared into the heavens, breaking out into beautiful coloured stars, or coloured rain. The marine rockets and the Very lights bursting among them was the most fantastic firework display I had ever seen; Crystal Palace was nothing to this. The sky was lit up with all the colours of the rainbow, and the noise sounded like El Alamein all over again. Needless to say, all hell was let loose in the camp. They thought the German army had come back and it was a full scale assault on the airfield. We saw the RAF Regiment gunners trying to bring their

A/A guns to bear in our direction, tracers were going in all directions when they woke up. We decided to make ourselves scarce, and disappeared stealthily through the woods like commandos to reach our hut. The whole place was in such an uproar no one took any notice of us. Fortunately in the dark nobody saw the disreputable state we were in. We had a hell of a job getting rid of grass, twigs and the smell of cordite before we all had a victory toast to a successful midnight sortie and collapsed in our beds with happy grins on our faces, despite the commotion outside. This was a happy time for me.

At 5 a.m. two of us got a rude awakening by an orderly, staggering off for breakfast I didn't know what day it was, I felt dreadful. Bert Woodman was in the same boat, he couldn't face bacon and eggs either. I don't remember how the transport driver got us aboard and dropped us at our aircraft in the dark, all I knew was that I felt terribly cold and wished my head would stop throbbing. My ground crew soon lifted me in the cockpit and strapped me in with the usual wisecracks. One put my helmet on and fastened the oxygen mask on my face and turned it on full blast, telling me to breathe deeply. I hadn't the strength to argue so humouring them I did as I was told.

After five minutes I began to feel I was back in the land of the living, I could distinguish the illuminated gauges without my eyes hurting. Fortunately when the Very light signalled our move to the runway – now repaired – the engine was running and I had marshalled my wits together. Taking deep breaths of oxygen – I hoped we weren't going to be flying much above 10,000 feet, otherwise I was going to be in dire trouble if I ran out of it – I took off into the gloom about 6 a.m., formating on the leader without incident and within 15 minutes I was my old self again. Medically speaking, it never ceased to amaze me that for years I could throw off the after-effects of over-indulgence very quickly, but that was in the days of hard physical training and adequate sleep. Since operational training and posting to 130 there was no time to spare for keeping fit and we always lacked sleep, but although we didn't drink to excess every night, I could still throw it off and cause no one any concern. No allowance was made for anyone for dereliction of duty due to drink; some officers who had thrown caution to the winds at times were very sharply reprimanded, for it endangered everyone flying with them. In the officers' mess it would be all too apparent of course, but that was when the sergeants' mess was a blessing for some chaps. I personally never had alcohol until flying was finished for the day, but made up for it in the evening.

As it happened, I was clobbered by anti-aircraft fire over Quakenbruck on our return from our sortie to Bremen. The boss was gradually losing height on our homeward leg on a very pleasant evening, at a gentle cruising speed, when a barrage opened up at short range. We were in close formation and an easy target, but I was the only one to collect some shrapnel before the squadron could spread out. It wasn't much to speak of, fuel tanks and the engine weren't hit and I had her under control, but if the gunners had been German we would have suffered much more damage; the culprits were American! Intelligence bods had told us at briefing that Quakenbruck was taken by the Yanks, so the boss didn't expect this reception from our trigger-happy allies, otherwise he would have given it a wide berth.

On landing at base I hurried to our hut, but to my bitter disappointment, Johnny had gone. He left a note for me wishing us all the best of luck and thanking us for a night he would never forget. He was anxious to rejoin his squadron but he was sure we would meet again and in his vernacular which he used flippantly on occasion, '. . . Dinna fash yersell aboot me.' In other words – don't worry about me. 'I wish I could have been one of your outfit; you've a great bunch of lads there, and I know you will come through, so don't forget our date.' I never heard of him again.

He had told me Mitch was posted to another squadron of Typhoons, and Johnny to his great regret had lost contact with him. They were both in the same wing but his efforts to find him met with no success. Johnny thought he might have bought it early on, when as a newcomer his name wouldn't be well remembered. I never traced Sergeant Pilot Sandy 'Mitch' Mitchell either; I asked every Typhoon pilot and squadron we came across, but drew a blank. Mitch disappeared completely and that was the end of 'The Three Musketeers'. In 1946 I wrote to AM Records for information on my two mates, but they refused to help on the grounds that they only divulged it to next of kin or a near relative.

The bedlam of the night before was put down to saboteurs, much to our amusement. It was accepted that the countryside abounded with partisans, isolated Germans and Dutch sympathizers, but why they would bother to cause such confusion without any material gain was never explained by the brown jobs (army) intelligence corps.

Spitfire XIVs at 130 Squadron in Holland. The author is not present.

Above Focke-Wulf 190 at Celle.

Below Fairey Battles in Holland.

Above Captured Junkers with RAF roundels.

Below 'My mate Mike Ockendon, March 1945. Wizard bloke.'

The Me 262, the world's first operational jet fighter. Rheine, spring 1945.

IX

The Last Lap

Relations amongst us were considerably jollier than when I first joined the squadron, I had one victory to my name and returning from another sweep I damaged a BF109G fighter in a little skirmish over the airfield. It became apparent that when I first appeared on the scene, the old system I had experienced in my recruit days still applied. In those days one was always being told to 'get some in' (a reference to one's lack of long service). The analogy here applied to flying hours, and the lack of them. Time serving airmen, (regulars) were always treated with suspicion by 'hostilities only' officers and men, who considered themselves superior in intellect to the regulars. Few regulars volunteered, and those that did were seldom accepted for active service so late in the war. My colleagues were direct entries in the aircrew category, albeit late entries, and knew nothing of the basic airman's life. Consequently there had always been this barrier, until I had proved myself and Johnny's illuminating appearance on the scene had redressed the balance – disclosing more about my service than I had ever volunteered. My adopted extrovert attitude may have given cause for some doubt of their own abilities, but it was self-defence on my part.

We were frequently visited by Harry Broadhurst, our Group commander, in his little German Fieseler Storch air observation aircraft, which he had acquired some time ago for his own personal use to communicate with his units. It bore the roundels of the RAF of course but many times it was mistaken for an enemy aircraft, and he had some hairy moments flying over Allied anti-aircraft units who opened up on him. I liked him immensely. There was no side with him and he always found time to talk to the NCO pilots. His record spoke for itself, he led a wing from 12 Group against the onslaught of the Luftwaffe attacks in the earlier days of the war. His elevated rank of air vice-marshal hadn't changed him. There were times though that squadrons had cause to curse him back at Eindhoven; he popped up out of nowhere to throw the air and ground controllers into a flap to give him priority to land, whilst a squadron was standing on the runway waiting to take off on an operation. Personally I blamed the controllers rather than him; his small high-winged monoplane could land within 50 yards and he didn't require a runway to land on; a patch of grass was adequate. He always flew it himself, carrying Montgomery, Eisenhower and on one occasion, the King himself.

The month of April was an extremely busy month for all of us. I personally flew 34 operational hours, flying twice a day most days – the average duration of a flight was 75 minutes due to the short range of the Spitfire – but within a few minutes of flying from our base, one was in the danger zone of the combat area. A number of days of bad weather prevented any flying, but when it permitted, sections of four or six aircraft flew sorties over different areas at the same time, or as one section landed another took off. The operations room flight board resembled a bus station timetable at times. For me, April was the most memorable month in the short time I had been with the squadron, I was in the thick of the fighting with them and as the uneasy days of March were left behind, I felt I belonged to the squadron. Every man was needed to double up.

A new member joined us on the 15th, Warrant Officer Fred Griffiths, another displaced pilot; taking the place of the absent George.

On 16 April 1945 the squadron was moved to Celle, its first base in Germany. The previous day, on a sweep over Bremen to Rethem, I scored a hit on a Ju188 engrossed in bombing a British supply convoy. One engine was on fire as she dived for the deck and flew over a German flak battery. They gave me a hot reception with everything they had; banking steeply I got to hell out of it. Porky's advice about rough usage of the rudder was invaluable in these circumstances, my aircraft appeared to be pointing in a straight line to the German gunners, when in fact it was skidding along another, thus fooling their line of sight. It was a relief to see the tracers lazily going by. Of course this was very deceiving – when one's aircraft is doing well over 450 mph head on, the tracers did appear to be coming at one slowly but suddenly they streaked past at a terrific velocity. When climbing away from it the tracer appeared to float lazily by. I doubt if the Ju188 made it back to base, but good luck to them if they did.

Opportunities for wingmen were very few and far between, but in the circumstances related above when this flock of 12 very fast ground-attack/bombers didn't have, or require, a fighter escort – everyone was allowed to join in and bag what they could. Three were shot down by our section of eight, splitting their formation up; when my chance came to latch on to this chap high-tailing it for his lines. Many were the times I wished I had a freelance role, but flying discipline was paramount.

The aerodrome was a luxurious pre-war Luftwaffe training establishment with modern accommodation in splendid buildings; murals on the walls; and crystal chandeliers hanging from the ceilings of the numerous messes, and even the toilets had an air of grandeur, carpeted, with huge mirrors decorated in gilt frames. The living quarters were far superior to any I had ever seen in the RAF, built in two-storey blocks, they contained single rooms with all the amenities of a three-star hotel, as classified in those days. They were the senior NCOs' quarters. The officers said they were astounded with their palatial quarters, which were of course far superior to ours. This base was the premier training base of Germany where all the aces had been trained; it far surpassed the Royal Air Force College at Cranwell or the army's college at Sandhurst. We flew in the day after the British Second Army spearhead reached it; to the south the Americans were advancing on a broad front whilst the main body of the British troops were pushing north and north-east to the Baltic coast where they met the Russians.

The domestic staff who cleaned the rooms and changed the bed-linen lived in flats above the buildings. They were mostly young girls, and it was remarked that they probably comforted the Luftwaffe in bed too.

The stuff-shirted commander of the army corps, who seemed to be in command of the base when we arrived, soon got rid of the domestic help, although they had nowhere to go; the town was in ruins. He threw all German civilians off the base, on the grounds that they were saboteurs and thieves. This was not only laughable but tragic for me. My treasured flying jacket disappeared from my room two days after they had gone, in the hands of one of his own mob when we all went to the mess for a meal. I knew it was true. He was seen running out of the billet with a leather flying jacket by one of the erks passing by, who thought it was odd, (it could not be mistaken for the type of sleeveless leather jacket the army wore) as our quarters were out of bounds to all other ranks, especially the army. The fighting

troops had moved on and this was the first time we had met the army
servicing and ordnance swaddies. They weren't to remain long.

I kicked up merry hell with the brown jobs on the station, but got
nowhere. I searched their trucks until I came across one with two
armed soldiers sitting in the back of one of them. I was told that if I
mounted the tail board of it, I would get my brains blown out. I've
refrained from naming the army corps by name, but shall we say they
were *not* front-line troops. They contained the dregs of the army in
my opinion; always in the rear, never in action, and the biggest
bunch of black-marketeers of all the services. They robbed the
British front-line troops with equal unanimity as they did the enemy.
One of the unsavoury facts of life in wartime was that certain factions
of the British and American forces were equally guilty of looting as
were the Germans, and equally as vicious in obtaining it, no matter
to whom it belonged. No one should be under any disillusionment
that the practice only applied to the rank and file either. The whole
business was both distasteful and sickening to me. I can say with all
honesty I was never involved in these criminal activities, but there
was nothing I could do about them. Depending on rank, some of the
transport aircraft's cargoes headed for the UK wouldn't bear
inspection.

Based at Celle brought us nearer the action at the front, the range
was reduced considerably and the air space was much smaller.
Consequently the Luftwaffe were more concentrated as they were
trapped between the Russians to the east and the British and
Americans in the west and south. Celle airbase was 80 miles short of
the Elbe and 140 to Berlin. The squadron and its companion
squadrons, 41 and 350, were soon joined by others and the airfield
became very busy with transport traffic using the airfield as it
became a repatriation centre for prisoners-of-war; but it was now
under the command of the RAF.

Operations took the squadron north and north-east of Hanover to
Hamburg, Lübeck along the Baltic coast, Schwerm, Uelzen,
Lüneburg and Perleberg. The area swarmed with FW190's and
ME109G's, but appeared to lack leadership. It was rather odd that
earlier, when we were at Eindhoven, prior to the last assault on the
Rhine, they were conspicuous by their absence. The only conclusion
was that some were at the Russian front and they were now
reinforced by squadrons brought south from Norway. The three

squadrons of 125 Wing were spread out to cover as much air space as possible, it came down to every man for himself. The Luftwaffe had nothing to lose but its self-respect. Consequently after intensive fighting they were overwhelmed by sheer exhaustion, lack of fuel, and short of ammunition. Individual actions of pilots of 130 Squadron were numerous.

On the sorties I flew I was fully occupied in keeping station on the leaders and the boss when he was free from other duties to lead us; flying above and behind him, whilst he was hell bent on scything the enemy down. After warning him of danger from behind, I had my hands full, cutting in and diverting any attack on him, hopefully blasting everything in my sights. One didn't have time to observe everything around us, I just did my job, but many times when I found myself in difficulties, the boss spotted it and smartly reefing round, he was behind my attacker forcing him to break off the action, much to my relief. It was a very brave man who tenaciously stuck to shooting down his enemy when he himself found he was the target, having his own tail blasted off, and there weren't too many of them on either side. We had little contact with the other two squadrons of the Wing, so we didn't know how successful they were.

One of the exasperating things of air warfare, was that one could fly one sortie after another, day by day, and never see a thing to shoot at, let alone an enemy aircraft. But other sections seemed to have all the luck, and bag something every time they were airborne, it was a game of chance. Many pilots' names were not recorded in the squadron's log because the dice was loaded against them, but they all tried to get in the action and played their parts magnificently as part of the team. Officers and men were bonded together in this, it was all a question of the luck of the draw.

After my early days in Holland – when I was anxious about my ability – I took a fatalistic attitude to life. It was no use worrying about tomorrow, there was no point in it; it got one nowhere. There wasn't any tomorrow, one had to live for the day. I laughed to myself when I recalled my training days, every little incident seemed to be the end of the world then. How childish we all were, to take life so seriously. I had suddenly grown up and could stand back dispassionately now. Everything was pre-planned in my mind and the future, was in the lap of the gods. Nobody knew when his number was up, so what the hell. The only thing to do was adopt a cavalier, carefree outlook on life, and enjoy the few hours after dinner until bed-time, preferably with a glass in one's hand. Fortunately I wasn't married so I had no responsibilities to distract me.

In a section of four Spitfires on a sortie to Hamburg in the Schwerm area, I was hit in the undercarriage during an attack on a road convoy. Flying Officer Wilson checked that I couldn't lower it and I had to return to base. Reaching base I was ordered to use the emergency bottle to lower the undercart and lock it; fortunately it worked. It was a last ditch device using high pressure and never used except in extreme circumstances: once the lever was pressed if the undercart stuck halfway down, there was no way of raising it to belly land. The whole hydraulic system had to be stripped and cleaned out after use before repairs could be effected, and it didn't make one too popular with the ground crew.

In the evening of the 19th, Phil Clay was one of a section of four led by Flight Lieutenant Walmsley east of Hamburg when they ran into 20 plus E/A (enemy aircraft). The leader returned to base with engine trouble and Flight Lieutenant Ponsonby took over and gave chase. Phil and Flying Officer Murphy (Australian) were shot down over enemy lines. I had a distinct feeling that I had heard this story before, and was I glad I wasn't included in this one.

On 20 April the squadron flew five sorties in sections. I flew in two of them. On the first one of four aircraft led by Flight Lieutenant Walmsley we encountered eight FW190s. Between him and Flight Lieutenant Ponsford they shot down two with one probable and two damaged. We were bounced from behind. I was caught in the initial attack by the Luftwaffe fighers and sustained damage to the rudder which put me out of the action. On the last sortie of the day in the evening in a section of six led by Flight Lieutenant Samouelle, he shot down two Focke-Wulf FW190s.

Reading up the histories of the early fighter pilots and their accredited victories, I envied them the chance to shoot down virtually unarmed bomber and transport aircraft. They provided invaluable practice in judgement of range and deflection, for when they met the more adept enemy fighters; thus learning how to add to one's score and becoming a recognised ace, in the eyes of the press and public by their decorations.

I'd become aware that some pilots actually enjoyed the war, and as we were nearing the closing stages, their enthusiasm knew no bounds hunting for the odd enemy aircraft here and there who were trying to escape the net. Anyone looking at the list of individual pilot's scores would notice that the pilots with the highest scores always seemed to be in the right place at the right time and could be counted on two hands. The vast majority were lucky if they bagged one, but it wasn't any fault of theirs if they failed to register any victories at all.

Flight Lieutenant Walmsley, our flight commander, was promoted to squadron leader and posted to No 350 (Belgian) Squadron in our wing, on 24 April. He was a resolute fighter pilot who led his section with distinction and fully deserved his promotion and command. In this month alone he had accounted for a dozen enemy aircraft either killed outright or damaged. He took over from Squadron Leader Terry-Spencer who had led 350 since they lost their Belgian CO.

To recapitulate, Hanover was captured on 19 April; four days later the British took the town of Celle and the aerodrome, which the squadron occupied immediately it was declared cleared of mines and serviceable. The town was noted for its large railway junction and marshalling yards. The scene when we arrived was one of devastation, the marshalling yards and railway depot had been bombed out of existence with most of the town; the airfield however, was comparatively untouched. It was situated ten miles east of Hanover, where Field Marshal Montgomery established his head-quarters.

Three NCO pilots joined the squadron in this month: Flight Sergeant Seymour and, Warrant Officers Mould and Griffiths. We had lost two in Phil Clay and George Warren.

Towards the end of the month the recently joined Warrant Officer Miller bought it when he was shot down in flames by the rear gunner of a Junker 188 (fast medium bomber) during his attack on it. Usually rear gunners were ignored but this one I'll bet, couldn't believe his luck. This very experienced Australian warrant officer had been with us less than a month and we barely knew each other. Such was squadron life now.

On 23 April a certain Rhodesian flying officer joined the squadron, a nondescript character to arrive so late on the second front, one would have thought. He was a likeable chap to talk to on the few occasions I met him, but there was something out of the ordinary about him; he was an intellectual with firm ideas. He entered the service as a sergeant, flew with the Desert Air Force and was injured. After hospitalisation he resumed flying from Corsica and was shot down again over Italy, but with the aid of the local populace he eventually made his escape. Determination on his part took him to England nearly a year later, to continue the fight, and after conversion at the same old 83 GSU, Dunsfold, we all knew so well, he arrived at 130. This man, although no one could possibly envisage it then, was to be the future Prime Minister of Southern Rhodesia and eventually kicked in the teeth by the ruling British government for his pains – he was none other than Ian Smith (service number SR80463).

Important prisoners arrived by road and light aircraft from Hanover and American headquarters, day by day to be transported by Dakotas to various British and American judicial units, for interrogation by senior Intelligence officers. Amongst them were the notorious SS custodians of the concentration camps, of which we had only recently become aware. The heavy transportation traffic out of the airfield consisted of British and American prisoners-of-war who arrived by the truck load every day. Lancasters, Liberators and Dakotas arrived and departed in a constant stream, empty inwards; but fully laden, outward-bound for the UK.

We commandeered a German half-truck and went to Belsen to see for ourselves what the situation was, none of us had believed what we had heard. The army tried to keep us out, but we were determined to let nothing stand in our way, after a hairy road trip involving a skirmish with an isolated German army unit. It was our first action on the ground, with a fixed German machine-gun mounted on the vehicle and a few belts of ammo and with the assistance of a few British troops on the road, we fought them off. Mick Coverdale took command of the machine gun. As fast as I could feed the ammunition belt in, he emptied it. He was most upset when the action was over and we still had some ammo left. Fortunately none of us were hit, I shuddered to think what the reaction of the boss would have been if anyone was a casualty, but we realised our scene was in the air. The amused comment from the troops was, 'You blokes can look after yourselves all right.' Belsen was unbelievable; it is history now, everyone knows the horrific facts, but to innocents like ourselves, the sight and smell made an indelible impression. We saw it as it really was. How any man could commit such perpetrations was simply beyond us; we wished we had known a few months earlier.

We got a rocket from an army staff officer for our little escapade, and were confined to the camp from then on. In retrospect I suppose it was stupid when we didn't know the overall picture. He told us that the Germans were still very active in the district, small bands were mining roads at night; even the base service roads came under attack. Dispatch riders were cut in two by these commandos, lying in wait in the woods; by stretching wires across the road when they saw them approaching. It took time to clear out these isolated pockets.

The NCO pilots were lucky, we were still six strong with replacements, we had only lost three, but officers were constantly replaced for one reason or another: consequently we never really got to know them as real comrades. For some time we had a preponderance of flight lieutenants, so much so, I for one lost track of who were the flight commanders. It would seem everyone wanted to be in at the death, and of course influential rank counted a great deal. They were complete strangers to us. It was a great pity we didn't miss them when they disappeared from the scene, but how could we – until their absence was obvious. If there was one criticism I would make against the system existing then, it was the failure of senior officers to attempt to consolidate social relations between officers and NCOs. Rank was of no consequence in the air, except that it counted when choosing who they flew with, certain cliques of them always flew together. I never knew any of them try to pull rank on an NCO at any time but then they didn't have any cause to and they had the commonsense not to rock the boat if they thought there was.

All the NCO pilots felt this keenly, especially those who were leaders of sections in earlier times and gradually displaced by new officers. Fighter pilots had the reputation of being loners, as opposed to bomber pilots, but there was nobody more a loner than the lowest rank on a fighter squadron in 1945: it was a far cry from 1939/40. Memories were very short.

Johnnie Johnson issued a bulletin declaring the wing score of enemy fighters shot down in the month of April as 38, congratulating all three squadrons on this achievement. We saw little of him around the squadron dispersal; he would have been a popular figure if he had taken time off to talk to the NCOs, but as it was, we only saw him a few times in a Spitfire. I flew with him three times as his wingman but he wouldn't be aware of my identity, I only met him face to face on one occasion and never informally.

Phil Clay and Flying Officer Murphy, another Aussie, survived the action of 19 April and were taken prisoners. They were liberated by the Americans and were welcomed back on the squadron. Murphy, was sent home, his days in the service were over. Phil claimed he was shot down after he had destroyed a FW190 on that fateful day. He was awarded the DFM on the strength of his five kills, the accepted figure for an award as a general rule, unless some exceptional flying valour warranted it.

Phil had applied for his commission, but he never received it. It was noticeable that colonial senior NCOs were commissioned in a very short time but British NCO pilots had little success. All our colonial mates received them eventually, even after the war ceased, but they were posted elsewhere. We lost three Australian NCOs in action. The colonial governments were generous to their own people, and appreciated the fighting qualities of their own pilots.

About this time, the strain began to show, we knew the war couldn't last much longer. I for one, found myself listening to the beat of the engine and suddenly noticed how rough it was running – it was no different to what it always had been – but imagination played a large part. All the odd noises became more apparent, noticing the slightest deviation of pressures and temperatures on the gauges, checking and re-checking the controls. All of which a pilot should normally do, but as one's operational duties fully occupied one's mind, one ignored the little vagaries and got on with the job; otherwise the ground crew would have had every aircraft grounded! No one spoke or gave any indication of his feelings, morale was high, conversation turned for the first time – except those who were happy to continue the war for ever – to going home and discussing everyone's hopes for a successful peacetime future. Nevertheless there existed some disquiet and I am not ashamed to admit, I for one, was getting the *twitch*, and I have every reason to believe that I was not alone: although none of us would ever admit it.

It would have been quite in order, to have a word with the MO and express one's feelings, but one avoided the medical fraterntiy like the plague. The net result would be a posting home, demoted back to the lowest rank of AC2 and given a broom to clean the ablutions with. In other words, disgraced. It could only happen to an NCO; if one was absolutely 'bomb-happy' he was a hospital case, but if one had any self-respect he soldiered on and kept his feelings to himself. Officers could not be demoted nor lose their commission.

Their psychological cases were treated as highly confidential, consequently none of the lesser mortals ever learnt the fate of these officers, but it was suspected that they were rested indefinitely. No such comfort for the NCO pilots, although they may have been on operations for a long time.

The Royal Air Force could not deprive an NCO of his 'wings'. They were his own personal achievement; he was a pilot and nobody could take that away from him. The whole situation put the RAF in a bad light; they were without doubt guilty of disgraceful conduct towards patriotic aircrew who had put their lives in jeopardy for their country. Instead of being treated as heroes – as the Americans did – they had the ignominy of reading on their permanent record in red ink: LMF (lack of moral fibre). This iniquity ruined many men's lives in peacetime, not to mention the scorn that was heaped upon them by the ignorant, jealous morons of lower order airmen, whilst they were still in the service. They were easily picked out with their brevie still on their tunics but with their chevrons removed. No longer respected by anyone. It may have been the policy of the RAF to deter pilots from going sick. If so, it succeeded. How could anyone return home in disgrace to face his family and friends, and the whole world in fact. Many chaps stuck it out and died needlessly as a result.

The three powers had decided to draw a line of demarcation at the river Elbe, the Western Allies could have reached Berlin long before the Russians, but the US First and Ninth Armies were halted and had to remain on the west bank of the river.

The Russian army had not yet taken Berlin. They were held up by the fierce defence of the Berlin garrison for nearly a fortnight. They didn't meet up with the western armies at the Elbe until 3 May, seventeen days after the British and Americans were halted and prevented from getting to Berlin. Our fighters had cleared the north and north-eastern Germany far beyond Berlin over the Russo-German front line, without any sign of the Russian Air Force and in the south the USAAF fighters had kept pace with us.

The squadron's operations were now directed eastwards in a direct line to the city of Berlin, whilst the politicians planned everyone's destiny. We met furious opposition from the remnants of the crack Luftwaffe fighters over the remaining 140 miles, but it was short-lived. The three squadrons were now flying in larger formations, sometimes led by Wing Commander George Keefer, the wing leader, and sometimes by the CO of the wing (Group Captain

'Johnnie' Johnson) flying with us as a flight commander. I flew in my usual position as wingman to the leader with 34 Spitfires behind me on occasions, a comforting thought for me as well as the leader.

Johnnie Johnson was hard to contain when enemy fighters were sighted; he banged open his throttle through the gate and a slight delay in following suit left one miles behind especially if one was flying an elderly hard-flown aeroplane.

The Luftwaffe fighters were few in number now and the actions were few and far between. They were deployed in last ditch and very successful attacks on the US Eighth Air Force Fortress's last bombing raids on Berlin using the fighter version of the jet-engined Me262. The weight of the RAF fighters took their toll and it was all over for the German Air Force before the USAAF fighters Thunderbolts and Russian Yaks and Migs joined in to make a nuisance of themselves.

Field Marshal Montgomery was kept busy during this time accepting the surrender of the German commanders of the north and north-west armies that were circumvented, taking 150,000 prisoners, by 4 May. Without doubt he could have crossed the Elbe and taken Berlin before the Russians or the Americans if politics hadn't forbade it. His war ended at Hannover.

No 130 Squadron continued on reconnaissance sweeps to Berlin; thousands of refugees were fleeing before the Russians, choking the roads westwards, unfortunately they included hundreds of deserters. For some reason not explained to me, action had to be taken against these unarmed troops – some out of uniform – mingling among the civilian columns which also contained thousands of forced foreign labourers such as the Ukrainians. I could not derive any enjoyment from literally murdering women and children, it was impossible to avoid them and their few pets and belongings, the German troops were indistinguishable from the civilians and knew how to take cover, but one couldn't argue. I knew of course that the Luftwaffe had no mercy on civilian refugees when they were driving towards the coast in the first years of the war, but I had no desire to be tarred with the same brush. I thought I was more civilised than the bloody Germans although I hated them as much as the next man. The hypocrisy of various aces on each side giving credit to each other and actually fêting them, was sickening. Galland and others were treated – even after the war – as heroes by well-known RAF fighter aces, and embraced as brothers of the air. This sort of thing brought the fighter-arm into disrepute among bomber crews and troops; they were not to know that the average fighter pilot had no sympathy with the Luftwaffe glory boys and the British aces who fêted them.

I was reprimanded when the films (taken when the firing button was pressed) were shown that night. Mine showed that most of my ammunition passed over the heads of the mass of people as I levelled out from the dive, and not in the dive. My excuse was that I had forgotten to release the safety-catch on the trigger and realised it too late. The boss had no comment apart from observing it was a lousy shooting and he hoped, with his tongue in his cheek, that it hadn't happened before. I didn't see the film, I didn't want to; one happy limitation of being a bomber pilot was that he didn't see the face of someone he has just killed, but they were very vivid to a fighter pilot on an open road. It was an experience I'll never forget. The enemy was remote in air-to-air combat; he was a machine bent on destruction; it was one's job to permanently prevent that whatever the cost to human life, but killing unarmed civilians, I had no stomach for. Perhaps psychologically, I was not the aggressive pilot the RAF thought I was, but strictly speaking I had to be motivated. I have mentioned before during this narration of my career in the service, that I could be aggressive if challenged or angry – I had plenty of experience fighting the hierarchy and not afraid of the consequences – but I didn't have the indiscriminate, blood-thirsty, killer instinct of some pilots who evidently had an abundance of it; whatever the circumstances were. I was happier in the days when it was a question of the other chap or me.

More satisfactory and exciting moments were the encounters with the Russian Yak–9 fighters, constantly bouncing the wing like a swarm of bees. It was good tactical practice, exhilarating disciplined flying at its best. Our leader, judging the timing to a nicety, easily kept us out of trouble. It was infuriating for the Russians to be outmanoeuvred and they became more aggressive. They ultimately found themselves absolutely outclassed, especially with their inferior aircraft. They really were a dreadful rabble. The top brass decided to curtail the Berlin trips; it was getting too dicy. There might have been an unfortunate accident resulting in another war on their hands. The Reds had finally taken Berlin on 2 May and considered the territory theirs, resenting our presence. They suffered tremendous losses on the Eastern front it is said; hardly surprisingly, witnessing their tactics, and equipment. They were far inferior to the

Spitfire Against the Odds

Luftwaffe fighter pilots of the earlier years, making up their lack of skill by sheer aggression and numbers. But the wholesale reduction of flying schools and the dissipation of their operational training aircraft by sending them to the front-line squadrons with poorly trained pilots lowered the status of the Luftwaffe. Thousands of bomber pilots had to be converted to fighters, but the experiment proved worthless. To make matters worse Hitler brought experienced combat commanders out of the line and gave them staff jobs for which they were unsuited. If Hitler had spent more money on development and production of fighters rather than bombers when the tide turned against him, his pilots would have had a fighting chance.

The war on the Russian front was won on the ground of course, where life was cheap and the weather played the biggest part. A Luftwaffe pilot taken prisoner at Celle told me that they couldn't get aircraft based at forward airfields off the ground in the winter of 1943/44, although anti-freeze was used extensively. The engine, fuel pipes and the oil in the sumps froze solid; the control surfaces couldn't be freed of ice and even had difficulty moving them on the ground. It was impossible to operate from forward bases to stop the hordes of Russian troops advancing until the spring when it was too late.

The war in the air had virtually ceased, but the Russian army was still waging a battle in the city. Operations petered out, only odd sections were still flying at the beginning of May. They were my last sorties in Germany, although some pilots were still looking for blood and formed freelance sections flying around in the hopes of finding something to shoot at.

On 7 May the nucleus of the squadron moved to Fassberg a few miles north of Celle on a ferry flight, where they were to say goodbye to their beloved combat Spitfire Mark XIVs and re-equip with No 411 Squadron's old Spitfire Mark XIX fighter-bombers. 411, a Canadian squadron, was disbanded and sent home. Our aircraft were handed over to a fighter-reconnaissance unit to continue flying as part of the British Air Force of Occupation.

I was scheduled a rest period and stood down, to await transport to go on leave, even if the war had continued.

The next day hostilities ceased, an anti-climax in more ways than one. Reorganisation was the main theme, sadly 125 Wing was disbanded. Johnnie Johnson made the most of the situation; he wangled a trip to Copenhagen and according to his own words, given the task of organizing a fly-past for the Danish Royalty by AVM Harry Broadhurst. He picked No 41 Squadron (the oldest) not surprisingly, and flew to Kastrup, Copenhagen for the Danish victory celebrations. No 41 returned a week later and with 350 (Belgian) Squadron remained with the BAFO. No 350 was officially handed over to the Royal Belgian Air Force the following year. We never came into contact with 41 and never met any of its pilots.

No 350 was an absolute rabble of fliers, very tenacious and excitable. They acquitted themselves with glory, but discipline wasn't in their vocabulary. Under their previous Belgian CO they were uncontrollable as a unit. But what I liked about them was their devil may care attitude and no respect for rank. Their previous CO Terry Spencer, knocked them into shape, but psychologically he was one of them, subsequently they came to accept him as one of their own until he was sent home after being shot down over the Baltic and returned to his squadron badly burnt. I am sure they received Squadron Leader Walmsley with the same warmth.

Our future came as a shock when we learnt we were destined for Norway. A cleaning up operation of recalcitrant German fortified pockets and the surrender of all Luftwaffe aircraft and airmen was our next assignment. The war, to our disgust, was not yet over. We were looking forward to the time of our life, celebrations everywhere, reaping the rich rewards of the conquering heroes, but it was not to be. No 130 Squadron was officially accredited with 158 victories in combat since its re-formation, not including the countless damaged aircraft that never reached base or the stationary aircraft disabled on the ground; or the V1's. The official figure from 8 October (when 130 destroyed the first enemy fighter since joining the 2nd Tactical Air Force to VE–Day is 98 enemy aircraft destroyed, over 1,000 road, rail and river transports destroyed and numerous fortified positions wiped out or damaged. In this period the squadron lost five pilots killed, two missing, six taken prisoner-of-war (four were repatriated) and eight hospitalised not to return. Of course during that period the personnel continually changed as pilots were promoted and posted to other units, or sent on well earned rest periods after a tour of duty. It should be mentioned that the squadron's records were poorly kept before October; a number were missing when they were in Fighter Command and later after hostilities ceased. Figures for Operation

'Overlord' and the operations leading up to D–Day were unobtainable when I left the squadron.

I wangled a lift in an Anson back to the UK a few days before the squadron left Germany on 10 May for North Weald, a famous wartime fighter base situated on the outskirts of London. For me it was home James and don't spare the horses, for a much needed break, hoping VE–Day hadn't been forgotten yet. In my absence the squadron was reorganised, colonials repatriated, and others posted or discharged. When they were replaced the squadron did a conversion course on the Spitfire IXs at North Weald and all the aircraft were overhauled and smartened up. I was to regret I didn't get the opportunity to put some flying hours in on these aircraft, but such is service life, one takes it as it comes I suppose, as I will relate in the next chapter. Squadron Leader Frank Woolley must have thought I was quite capable of the next job I was given, or he overlooked the fact I had never flown this particular Mark before. That, I will never know.

X

Enforced Interlude

At the end of May, a telegram arrived ordering me back to North Weald. I was a little surprised. It was so close to the end of my service that I didn't think that I would be going to Norway with the squadron. I had reluctantly come to the conclusion that I would probably be posted to another unit on my arrival, and my days with the squadron were over.

The station was deserted except for a small maintenance staff. On enquiring from the guard-room where 130 Squadron was situated on the airfield, I was told there were no squadrons there, they had all gone. I contacted the SDO (Station Duty Officer) at the HQ buildings after an orderly had rousted him out of the mess and asked him what the score was – and with my tongue in my cheek – how was I to rejoin my squadron?

He said to find some accommodation and come back in the morning, whilst enquiries were made. Once again it appears I arrived at the wrong time; everyone was on leave except for a skeleton staff, and the mess was closed down. The only sleeping quarters were ghostly empty huts with no bedding whatsoever. A corporal did what he could, poor blighter, and rustled up some bedding and blankets, but I apologised, thanked him for his trouble and told him I couldn't possibly stay in that filthy scruffy hut. I cleared off to London and stayed at the Union Jack Club.

The next day, instructions left by my CO were found, I was to fly an aircraft left behind for repairs and rejoin the squadron wherever they were as soon as they were effected. This was the best news I could possibly have received. I was still on the squadron strength. But I had forgotten in the excitement of finding a job awaiting me that it had changed over to the Mark IX from the XIV. I had no knowledge whatsoever of this aircraft. I couldn't even find a handbook on it. I went over to the maintenance hangar to find it and expected it to be in a serviceable condition. I gave the cockpit the once-over. It was different to my old aeroplane and I dared not ask too many questions, otherwise it would have given the game away that I had never flown this aircraft before. Consequently I would not have been allowed to take it, and I might have been held back and posted elsewhere – that had to be avoided at all costs.

Grabbing a fitter I told him I was going to air-test it. He went into a flap, he said he didn't think anyone still wanted it and nothing had been done. I told him to pull his finger out and get on with it or there would be hell to pay. My CO expected his full complement of 18 Spitfires and not 17. The aircraft had all been repainted and the squadron identification letters (AP) replaced the Canadians'. The squadron had been reorganised. Most of the Commonwealth pilots including Ian Smith were sent home. After familiarization flights on this different mark of Spitfire, the rest had a short leave before going north. I had missed them by a day.

After lunch the fitter said he thought AP–V was serviceable. I said OK I would take her up to make sure. It was quite the worst aircraft I had ever flown from the moment of take-off: it took the whole of the runway to gain flying speed, the power was nil, it was rough, mistimed. The gauges in the cockpit were unreliable, lights winked on when they should have been off, and vice versa. Added to that the controls were as sloppy as hell. I had to dig deep into my memory of the Spitfire Mark V's recommended figures for boost and adjustments of pitch – the combat Spitfires (Mark XIV) we had flown were automatic and although this one was supposed to be the first mark to have these advantages (Mark IX), they didn't work, so it was back to basics. It was more powerful than the early Spitfires but not as powerful and updated as the XIV. On landing, I told the fitter that I could not sign the form 700 (declaration that the aircraft was serviceable) and told him to get cracking on the faults. I could put up with the poor rigging which was hard work to keep her straight and level, but the engine had to be sorted out and new plugs and magnetos fitted. I could only guess the correct boost and cruising speed of this aircraft. I asked him if he had ever worked on a Merlin engine before. His reply was in the negative. North Weald was a famous fighter station in the Battle of Britain, but apparently he wasn't around then. Of course any fitter worthy of the name could tackle any engine; it was obvious to me he was just a flight mechanic not trained to the standard of a fitter. I told him I wanted it serviceable for the next day even if he worked all night.

Another night in the bright lights of the city didn't thrill me. I was very much alone. Strangely London had no attractions for me now: there was a time even in the blackout when I would have given my eye-teeth for leave in the great city but now I was lost and fed-up to the back teeth. Everything had changed; ingratiating strangers in a bar got short shrift from me. Most of the servicemen I met had never been out of the country – the fighting men were still on their way home – and the place was lousy with Yanks based in England throughout the war. I had to ration the beer too which was devastating. I had to have a clear head for the next day's trip north and I had a strange feeling I would need to be on top form.

The following morning I went straight to the hangar to be told that I would be better advised to leave matters over the weekend. They had done some work but the station would be fully manned next week. I saw the Duty Officer and told him as things stood it was not satisfactory, I would make a full report to my CO of the ineptitude of the staff when I rejoined the squadron. They were waiting to take a full squadron to Norway as a task force I reminded him, and his stationmaster (CO), would probably hear from the AOC 88 Group (Norway), to which we had been transferred. The war was not over for us, I reminded him.

He assured me that he would ginger up the ground crew. He didn't understand what all the panic was about, but he realised I had a strong case and he was temporarily in charge of the station. He wasn't used to a sergeant pilot laying the law down, but maybe it was to my benefit on this one and only occasion; a junior officer might not have had the gall.

After lunch, nipping back to the hangar like a praying mantis, I told them to make ready for another air-test. Off I went, the engine was more on song than it was but she was still staggering around like someone the worse for drink. However, I had no desire to stay over at this dump. I was just a visiting sergeant pilot who was a pain in the neck to the permanent staff, upsetting their weekend arrangements. They would be glad to see the back of me. I never realised before how much I missed the bonhomie of the squadron.

I doubted if this aircraft would ever be in a fit condition to fly to Norway but I must get back with the boys in case the whole thing were scrubbed and I found myself without a unit. Landing and taxying to the control, I signed the form 700 and told them I would land at RAF Thornaby to refuel before proceeding to Aberdeen. So at 1435 hours 26 May I took off for the north and how I was to regret it! Not just the immediate future but for the rest of my life. A strong will can also be a curse as well as an asset.

I had visions of beating up the old home town on my way and maybe stopping off at Millfield or Charterhall for a night at home if I got a move on. All went well for the first ten minutes then she began to be bloody awkward. Not to bore the reader with technicalities which would take too long to explain, it is sufficient to say I couldn't get her to cruise comfortably; I was constantly adjusting the propeller pitch or throttle setting to maintain an economical cruising speed the higher I went. I couldn't get her stabilized, for the automatic connection of the two wasn't working. I found the best altitude was 3,000 ft to fly straight and level. Then she started to yaw to port and drop the port wing. Hurriedly trimming the rudder to take the strain off my right foot and holding the wing up with the stick, I wondered what the hell had happened now. Everything looked normal except for dragging one wing so I was completely unaware of why the aircraft was such a brute to fly until a friendly Spit flew alongside and dropped his undercarriage to tell me something was wrong with mine. I couldn't believe it so I checked by dropping the undercarriage and lifting it a few times, no indicator lights showed and the horn didn't sound off when I throttled back – a warning that one's undercarriage is up when landing.

After take-off from North Weald the undercarriage had retracted OK but hadn't locked, although all indications showed it had; subsequently one leg dropped as the hydraulic pressure began to fail. There was no means of telling if it was an electrical fault or if the other one was locked up.

It became increasingly obvious the battery was going flat; the red light that indicated generator failure came on to tell me it wasn't charging the battery so I was in a quandary. I wondered why the Spit pilot hadn't called me on the radio. It was dead. Radios had been the bane of my life. But I had been through all this before and I refused to let it worry me. At least I didn't have to keep looking over my shoulder. When the faults became more apparent I had covered more than 100 miles and passed the Wash on my starboard side. There was no point in turning back. The temperatures were high and it was obvious I was using too much fuel even cruising as slow as 210 mph, which I had to guess was a reasonable cruising speed in comparison with the other marks of Spitfire.

If I could make Thornaby-on-Tees, I hoped they could sort it out; there would be the difficulty of getting both legs of the undercart down and locked, without using the emergency bottle. This would have held me up for days whilst the system was cleared. I would worry about that when I got there. I had my hands full battling with this cantankerous aeroplane.

Over the Humber to my utter astonishment the engine spluttered and cut out. My God, I thought, surely she hadn't used 92 gallons already after only 42 minutes' flying. I checked the fuel gauge but nothing registered for either tanks, switching over to the reserve 30 gallon drop-tank brought no response: I then realised that if I wasn't short of fuel, I had an air-lock in the system caused by vaporization or a fuel leak. There was no point in having an inquest at that moment. I hurriedly adjusted the trim of the aircraft to put her nose-down and keep flying speed. One doesn't have a great deal of time in these circumstances to check everything, when one is losing height at a rate of knots, and trying to prevent the aircraft from stalling and going into a spin. Recovery with the added complication of the drag of one leg hanging down, would have meant curtains for sure.

The Humber is a very wide river, 1½ miles wide upstream near Brough where the engine packed in and much wider towards the mouth. I didn't fancy baling out into the drink, for I had no mae west, blithely thinking I wouldn't need one on this trip, when I marked off the course on my maps. Not knowing the wind speed and direction, I would have looked a right stupid clot to be blown into the river to drown. Baling out never appealed to me anyway at any time, so that was out. I circled from the north side where I couldn't see any likely spot for a soft landing – it was too hilly and industrial – and back across the river; the south bank was my only hope. I'd lost height to 600 ft and luckily spotted a field alongside and parallel with the river. It would have to be a belly-landing of course. Having made my mind up, I switched off everything to cut down the risk of fire on landing, and jettisoned the 30-gallon slipper fuel tank.

I took a risk on this one field. It looked a bit short, but it was the flattest, a farmhouse and barns were directly in the way of the approach to it on one side, but I hadn't the height to round to the other end, and the next field was full of cows. It looked level because it had been cultivated, and crops were growing in it. I didn't notice the dry drainage ditches, they looked like access paths. Once a pilot

makes up his mind about his course of action, there is no going back
on it. For a fleeting moment my mind went back to Ismailia, as I
nursed this wreck above stalling speed up the river with one eye on
the farmhouse on the port side; I daren't undershoot and end up in
the farmer's bedroom. Banking sharply to the left in a U-turn I had
to build up the speed to over 140 mph in a dive for the approach to
the field. With fingers crossed, I selected flaps down to check the
speed when I knew I would make it – they act like an air brake and
alter the whole trim of the aircraft, especially with a dead engine not
to forget the dangling leg – and they worked. Unfortunately there
was a wind speed behind me of 15 mph or so which increased the
ground speed to 155 mph, but heading straight for a gap between the
farmhouse and barns I levelled off and we were through. As she sank
I noticed the field had a slight camber towards the river, holding her
off as long as possible at nought feet we hit the deck at about 95 mph
like a whale down a chute.

The next thing I remember was coming to, and wondering what
on earth I was doing here. The harness had slipped on impact and
my head had hit the gunsight immediately in front of me, splitting
my head open. I don't know how long I was out but when I pulled
myself together, I scrambled out of the cockpit and sat on the wing
that was still attached to the mainplane. Apart from the starboard
wing sticking up in the air, the Spit was lying quite peacefully,
straight and level, but with a large ditch under her nose. I was then
aware of the presence of an excited farmer and some young kids
prancing around. They were a bloody nuisance. The farmer was out
of his depth. He kept saying, 'Your face is covered in blood,' as
though he was demented. Stupid ass, a wet patch on his crutch was
evidence that he had pissed himself, (strange how one notices some
little irrelevant thing like that when otherwise not in possession of
one's faculties), the dirty old man.

Another chap came panting on the scene to tell me he had seen the
whole thing from the river. The plane had skidded along until the
nose dropped into the ditch and she reared vertically and when she
looked like going over on her back she dropped back again; the
starboard wing hit the bank breaking it off at the root at the same
time. Thank God she didn't go over on her back. I couldn't have
been unconscious for much more than four minutes, according to the
onlookers. A trail of unearthed turnips, like cannon balls scarred the

field. I asked this chap to give all the details to the law, who arrived in the shape of a fat rural police sergeant . . .

The sergeant was another moron, I thought he was going to ask me for my driving licence when he produced his little black note-book. I asked him where the ambulance was and he said we'll have you attended to when you have answered a few questions, sir. With that I exploded and marched off to the road where his land-rover was parked and told his driver to take me to hospital immediately, otherwise I would have his guts for garters. It sounds absolutely incredible, but it is the truth. I thought I was in a dream world; what they would have done had I still been in the aircraft mortally injured is beyond my comprehension. My trauma wasn't at an end.

Arriving at a civilian hospital at Scunthorpe, I was told to wait in the out-patients department! Clad in flying boots and a helmet stuck to my head with congealed blood I told the nurse I wanted to see the doctor right away. She said, 'You'll have to wait your turn.' I sat there for I don't know how long and passed out. When I recovered consciousness a doctor was leaning over me and he said, 'You should not have been brought here, the nurse thought you had been involved in a brawl; she didn't know you had crashed in an aeroplane.' I told him she didn't ask me. I had demanded to see a doctor which she refused, and I thought it was obvious to anyone with a grain of commonsense; even the patients were more concerned than she was.

To cut a long story short, a RAF ambulance eventually arrived, it was now four hours since the crash. These transport men were not medical orderlies and were annoyed at being called out on a Saturday evening and couldn't care less about me. On the way to some RAF station in Lincolnshire, they stopped at a pub and asked me if they could make a telephone call. I said certainly if they weren't too long about it, they arrived back an hour later, it would appear – I didn't know, I had passed out. I came to as we arrived at the station gates.

At the sick-bay a worried medical officer met the ambulance and asked, 'Where the hell have you been?' I told him to ask the ambulance drivers. He whisked me into bed and administered a morphine injection which put me out until the next day. After a long sleep I found my head was stitched up and bandaged, and clothed in clean pyjamas. The MO hurried in, looked into my eyes with some optical instrument and told me I was being transferred to RAF Hospital Rauceby for Aircrew. He said I was suffering from shock and concussion and may have a fractured skull and internal injuries. He thought it advisable to have a thorough examination. With that, out came his hypodermic needle and another shot in the buttocks.

I don't remember the 60 miles journey, but I was fully conscious on arrival at Rauceby near Cranwell. I was wheeled into the surgical ward to a bed already prepared with rubber sheets; it looked frightening. A sister rushed in and took one glance at me and laughed aloud, she said, 'Please excuse me, we thought you were a serious surgical case, I'm pleased to see it isn't the case. We won't need all this,' whipping rubber sheets off the bed. At last I had reached heaven, dozing and sleeping most of the time, after a week or so, I began to take in my surroundings and feeling ravenous, I had my first solid meals.

An investigation officer arrived and I gave a full report as much as I could remember, including the behaviour of everyone concerned.

The surgeon in charge told me I would be okay. He agreed with the diagnosis of the MO who had sent me there, but I hadn't a cracked skull or internal injuries apart from severe bruising and strained neck and shoulder muscles due to whip-lash. X-rays revealed no broken bones.

When I saw my fellow inmates for the first time, it came as a tremendous shock. I was simply horrified to see chaps with no faces, lips, eyebrows, eyelids, ears, and hair; what their bodies were like didn't bear thinking about. I was told by the sister that I was in the burns unit of Sir Archibald McIndoe, the pioneer plastic surgeon, and she knew I would have the courage to ignore what I saw, and to treat the patients as normal human beings. It gave me nightmares, but one had to overcome the natural repulsive feelings of seeing those masks with slits for the eyes and one for the mouth, two holes where their nose used to be and unable to use facial muscles. One had to get used to seeing these apparitions every day. It boosted one's morale to be in their cheerful company, nothing could equal their fortitude. They laughed inwardly with gurgling noises and joked about themselves, making me feel a fraud lounging around in hospital blue. I had seen many horrifying sights in the service, but there was no comparison to what was gathered here. This was the proud 'Guinea Pig Club' which was transferred later to a special plastic surgery hospital at Brighton, where his worked earned Sir Archibald a knighthood.

Taking a grip on myself I was determined to hide my feelings of nausea, but they weren't fooled, there was nothing wrong with their brains, they were a damn sight cleverer than I was. We spent many happy hours playing poker mostly; subsequently I lost more money than I could afford; I wasn't in their league, they were a right bunch of card-sharpers. They were going to spend many years of their life in hospital undergoing one operation after another to try to make them presentable to their families and the public as a whole. The local people of the village of Sleaford never gave them a second look on our outings to the local pub at lunch-times, they were to be congratulated on their sympathetic but tactful attitude, which made for a happy atmosphere.

The investigating officer revisited me a fortnight later, when I was up and about in my hospital blues (a bright blue civilian jacket and trousers with white shirt and red tie). He had a bulging brief-case with him this time. He told me the investigation had gone very well and he had all his evidence and I was absolved from all responsibility for the crash. Officially the Air Ministry accepted all responsibility. I should have been given technical instruction and taught the handling characteristics of the Spitfire Mark IX before flying it in any circumstances. He thought it was foolhardy to attempt the journey with an aircraft in such a poor condition though and I was at fault by pressing on. The board, however, recognized that I felt it was imperative that I did so in the course of my duty, and I was obeying orders. Evidence from the SDO North Weald supported that view, said the investigating officer when, looking through his documents he read the SDO's off-the-record statement 'he remembered the cheeky blighter who thought there was no tomorrow and seemed to think his squadron couldn't do without him . . .' With a huge grin he congratulated me for flying and landing the aircraft in such difficult circumstances.

By taking the aircraft apart the engineering investigation branch were able to verify my report, and, as he said, if I had baled out there might not have been any evidence left. Despite my ignorance the accident occurred through technical malfunctions; as a consequence certain disciplinary measures were being taken against various unnamed people for reasons he would not elaborate on, except that the transport ambulance drivers had been disciplined. With tongue in cheek, I said I had an aversion to water and it was my fourth prang so I was getting used to it. He shook his head; he was a technical officer and he seemed to have a great admiration for pilots. We shook hands warmly and he left wishing me the best of luck. I've no doubt he had my whole history among that huge file. The investigating branch were very thorough.

Three weeks later the deputy officer commanding the hospital, told me he thought I had recovered sufficiently to rejoin my squadron, but all aircrew had to be examined by a travelling medical board before being pronounced fit for flying. Unfortunately they were not due to visit Rauceby for another month and he could not discharge me. However instead of hanging around the hospital, he could authorise sick-leave until they returned, when I would be recalled for a thorough medical examination by members of the board. It was up to me he said. Well of course I asked – when is the next train for the north.

Before I left the boys decided to play a joke on me. In pre-war days the hospital was a mental hospital for civilians with numerous round padded cells. I was coerced to visit them by these bright lads and went inside one to satisfy my curiosity thinking they were behind me. Well, you've guessed it. As soon as I entered the cell the door was slammed shut. Believe me, I was never so frightened in all my life. It was a nightmare in this dreadful place with hidden pink lights; walls, floor and ceiling merged into one and after turning round, one didn't know where the door was. I never suffered from claustrophobia in my life, but at that moment I could have screamed with hysteria. After what seemed an eternity, but was in fact only a few minutes, the door opened. It would be wrong to say there was a row of smiling faces; they couldn't smile, but from their gurgles and antics they were hilarious with the success of their strategy of luring me into a padded cell. For all that I thought they were the greatest guys on earth, I was glad to get away to a saner world. I was given an affectionate send-off, hoping to see me on my return they said. They would plan a bang-on party and we would all get pissed. Amen to that I said, as we all shook hands and I boarded the little Commer for the railway station.

They gave me a new lease of life and I will never forget them. I didn't know it, but I was never to return to Rauceby.

Mother was surprised to see me so soon after my rest leave, but I didn't write to her, not wanting to alarm or worry her. In fact I don't think she knows to this day of my accident. I had a few blood-stains on my battle-dress, but apart from not being up to parade standard, it wasn't noticed unduly. I went into civies anyway, and was having a grand time with my old pals in the different services, as they all gradually returned home on demobilisation leave. It was a pleasant relaxation period for me, whilst I was wondering what the next RAF move would be, concerning my life. I was only a month short of my contract of seven years with the colours.

A lapse of memory troubled me – the period from the beginning of May until arriving home on rest leave is sketchy. I have filled in this fortnight from the information given me by my colleagues. I remember every detail of this last flight and the prang perfectly but I don't remember leaving Germany. There are no entries in my log after 24 April – but I know I flew until the end of the month. My log-book turned up when I reached Norway and was surprised there were no entries to jog the memory. Not keeping it up to date day by day had rebounded on me. This small lapse of memory still bothers me. I have no recollection of the journey home or the beginning of my leave during this period.

Mentioning this in later years to my civilian doctor he said it could have been due to shock and concussion of the accident, but he thought the amnesia was more likely to have occurred immediately after the event, wiping out the incident. However, circumstances may have brought it on due to delayed shock or even stress. I shall never know.

XI

Land of the Midnight Sun

Towards the end of July, a telegram arrived from 130 Squadron CO ordering me to report to Dyce. This was indeed a pretty kettle of fish. No orders to return to Rauceby, for a medical examination by the board had been received, and until I did, I was officially on sick-leave and grounded. I tried to contact the squadron at Dyce, but the airport authorities told me the squadron had left for Norway a considerable time ago. There was a small RAF administrative office there, but when given the facts they wouldn't involve themselves; they did not want to know about it, and had no advice to offer. Typical attitude of pen-pushers of course. I tried to contact the deputy CO at Rauceby, with the same results. He had gone on leave and the senior medical officer wasn't aware of the circumstances. I asked him for advice only to be told, 'Do your own thing, old lad.' The board had been and gone and wasn't due for another month. He didn't know why I wasn't called for the medical examination, but although my hospitalisation was recorded, no further action had been recorded. There was only one thing for it, to obey orders and go to Dyce.

The most exciting thing about the journey was that I travelled on the footplate of the engine, driven by my father to Edinburgh, where I changed to catch the Aberdeen express. It was indeed a privilege to ride on the engine and against all railway regulations, but Father took the risk and he knew his fellowmen would turn a blind eye. Very few people got the opportunity to travel on the main line in the cab of the locomotive unless they had a special pass, which was exceedingly hard to obtain. Railway historians will confirm the fact. It was an impromptu affair for which I was totally unprepared, otherwise I would have borrowed a pair of overalls and jacket from my father: he gave me no warning of his intentions the previous night.

I had to leave the footplate of the Gresley K3 at Portobello, the last stop before Edinburgh Waverley station – questions would be asked about me being on the engine by the station inspector, if I was still there – and I jumped in the first compartment of the first coach of the train which happened to be first-class.

A well-dressed middle-aged lady was the only occupant, she got the shock of her life when I entered – I didn't realise it but I was covered in greasy coal dust and stinking of smoke – I think she thought she was about to be assaulted by her expression. She was of the stiff upper-lip, haughty county class and although I explained I had been on the engine (I was in uniform but it didn't look like it after what it had been through since leaving North Weald and the stains added on the engine) she didn't believe a word I said. I thought she was going to pull the communication chain but fortunately she didn't: the coach was a non-corridor. I was glad to get out at Waverley and when I told father and his mate of the incident, he laughed and said he wouldn't have stopped in the tunnel leading to the station for anyone, the gradient was so steep he would never have got started again.

Arriving at Aberdeen I took a taxi to Dyce airport to report in, but it was a waste of time. Civilian authorities had taken over the airfield and were in control. There was a fair amount of activity in the transport section. I went to the main building to ask about a flight to Norway but they brushed me off and referred me to a tiny RAF office well away from the central block. There was no one there and no accommodation, I had to return to Aberdeen and put up at a hotel at my own expense.

The next morning I reported back expecting matters to be put in hand to get me away but they weren't the least interested, in fact the surly attitude of the sergeant clerk conveyed the impression that I was a damn nuisance. I had to be heavy-handed with the RAF office staff and tell them that they had to pull their finger out and get me to Norway even if it was in a fishing boat. They said I had been routed wrongly, all RAF personnel now left for Norway from a transportation base in the south. In fact I had missed the boat according to them, to which I replied that I was obeying my last orders and they had to facilitate them.

The officer-in-charge, a penguin flight lieutenant about 45 years old, told me they had more important things to do than worry about me. I said right-oh, fair enough, but the longer he kept me dallying around the more he would have to answer for. 'What's the panic?' he said. 'Go and get yourself lost.'

I laughed in his face and told him that when he got his priorities in the right order, I would be obliged if he would let me know, I would rather have stayed at home. I was a serving airman and I was entitled to be catered for, if nothing else. There was no accommodation on the airfield for me; he didn't even organise that! I told him I would find my own and send him the bill. So I returned to Aberdeen and found after a great deal of hassle, somewhere I could put my head down. The post-war malaise had set in with a vengeance in this country, as I persisted for days trying to contact my commanding officer.

The family that gave me accommodation in Blenheim Terrace, Aberdeen, were extremely kind, with two married daughters and a child living with them. It was a huge terraced house in pleasant surroundings, and I found myself a baby-sitter for the young married couples whenever the whole family had a night out together. For this I was more than amply rewarded by the most wholesome food and a good bed. They took me on the town and it didn't cost me a penny – the old adage of Aberdonians being careful with their money was absolute rubbish. We had many parties in the house, the younger people were very popular, having dozens of friends. I rather think I was some sort of prize capture and they liked to show me off, a very embarrassing situation at times. They had my uniform cleaned and pressed, so I was presentable once again.

Nearly a fortnight after my arrival, a passenger flight was arranged to Gardermoen, Oslo. It was originally planned for me to fly a spare Spitfire IX over the North Sea in company with other spare aircraft for other airfields but this was abandoned, much to my relief. It was with disbelief that I heard of this plan, it was so incongruous to expect anyone to fly that distance still convalescing from a crash in an aircraft that I wasn't fully acquainted with, and no one to check it out. However it was dropped, for some reason the orders were rescinded. Providing an escort for one single aircraft wasn't on, no one was allowed to fly that distance over the drink alone, in one small aircraft.

After kicking my heels at Gardermoen for more than a week, and not allowed to leave the camp for a night in Oslo, I was picked up by a ferry flight and eventually arrived at Kjevic, Kristiansand. The delays and efforts to reach there had diminished my enthusiasm to reach the squadron, I realised that I wasn't as fit as I thought I was, nothing tangible, but the old self-assurance was lacking and I didn't know why I wasn't my old exuberant self. I thought that a new country would provide excitement and get the adrenalin pumping again, I thrived on excitement, but it had deserted me and I felt thoroughly browned off with everything.

The squadron was away up north on escort duties when I reported to the new adjutant, and it would be some days before they returned to base. There was nothing he could authorise for me to do, in the CO's absence. He didn't know of my existence. When the squadron left the United Kingdom for Norway they were at full strength of 18 aircraft and 24 pilots, so it was obvious their numbers had been made up by replacements. The last entry in the squadron's records concerning me was dated 26 May, where it recorded my last flight, after that it was a blank. I filled in time by acting as airfield controller, a Walrus air-sea rescue unit from 276 Squadron was based there with 130 and a few communications aircraft.

Norway of course is a magnificent, spell-binding, mountainous country with the craggiest coastline in the world, abounding in waterways from the smallest inlet to the tremendously long, wide fiords. Kjevic airfield lay slightly short of the head of a ten-mile long fiord, the mouth of which narrowed to a tiny inlet at Kristiansand, a medium sized port on the south coast. The town had little to commend it, contingents of enemy troops were still being shipped out and it bore all the hallmarks of a naval and garrison town with warships in the harbour and streets full of troops. For some unknown reason it was out of bounds to the RAF, but it wasn't worth the boat trip on the choppy water anyway. Roads were atrocious in this very hilly terrain, hairy bends, and steep gradients, putting miles on a journey; not to mention the treacherous surface of rubble and poor foundations due to the very severe winters.

The airfield was virtually isolated for leisure purposes, the nearest village Tveid, was miles inland and there was nothing there but a community hall; the only buildings on the field were maintenance hangars, workshops and a few administrative huts. Behind them was the brick station HQ and sick-bay. Living quarters, sick bay, stores etc. were wooden shacks and hutments scattered over the hillside. The Germans had built a picturesque sergeants' mess and car park on a hill overlooking the valley, but it was a fair walk from our sleeping quarters. Officers had a similar one a mile away and transport around the camp was an absolute necessity.

When 130 arrived back, I reported to the CO and he wanted to know where the hell I'd been. He was aware of the accident of course but when he left Dyce he fully expected me to turn up beforehand. He was astounded to learn that I only received his telegram the day before he left, and I was on sick-leave: furthermore I had not been discharged for further duty when it came. I was a bit annoyed and I told him straight that no provisions had been made at Dyce by him for my transportation to Kristiansand; somebody had the crazy idea of flying myself here in a spare aircraft immediately after sustaining injuries in a crash-landing, and after that fell through I had the devil of a job to get here. It was only due to my persistence I was here now. He looked distinctly uncomfortable after all my explanations, he in fact, had not sent the telegram to my home address, it was the new adjutant, who must have eventually learned from the hospital of my whereabouts. But I rather think he had expected me to bring a spare aircraft.

So much for communications. He said he had left specific instructions for me at Dyce before they left but he didn't say what they were. However, he commiserated with me about my prang and my efforts to reach the squadron and welcomed me back to the fold. He was disturbed to hear I had not been pronounced fit for flying and said he would investigate the circumstances.

One of the golden rules in training, was to immediately send a pilot up again after an accident to restore his confidence if he was uninjured, but of course it did not apply to an experienced pilot or an injured one. Nevertheless in my case the gap was more than two months since I flew so I was anxious to take off and regain that sparkle.

When I walked into the mess I received stares of astonishment, I was surrounded immediately with a barrage of questions. They wanted to know where the prodigal son had been. Innuendoes were rife, the crafty beggar had been living it up in the flesh-pots of London and dodging the column. I was the butt of jokes for some days but after a while it was droppped when it wasn't funny any more. Bonhomie abounded. I was happy to be back among them again. They were my family, but I wasn't the old devil-may-care Ashy they had come to know with a certain amount of affection, since the halcyon days of Johnny's visit and the mad, mad consequences. One pleasant surprise was the presence of George Warren whom I last saw three months ago. He was injured crash-landing after his engine failed during that attack on the enemy armoured column, but

Pushing into Germany.

The original NCO pilots of 130 Squadron seen at Kristiansund, Norway, after VE Day, still operational. The Mark XIV Spitfires were left behind at Celle in exchange for the Canadians' Mark IXs.

Phil Clay DFC BEM in Norway with 130 Squadron.

Roy Coverdale in Norway with 130 Squadron.

Spitfire Mark IX AP–F. 'Before the crash at Kristiansand when I ran off the end of the runway on to the beach of a fiord in September 1945 when the brakes failed. . .'

After the crash. 'She dropped 30 feet from the runway to the beach breaking her back in two places.'

Above Flying Officer Sibley (from a damaged original).

Above A visit from King Olaf of Norway.
Below Norwegian motor patrol boats.

spent his time as a prisoner-of-war in hospital and rejoined the squadron in my absence.

The boss was concerned that I hadn't had a medical board, he had to cover himself of course, so he sent me to the station MO for an examination. Flight Lieutenant Morwood gave me a cursory check and said I was physically fit, so far as he could judge, but he had no X-ray equipment and injuries to the spine and head should be examined by specialists who were members of the Medical Board. He was not qualified to give an opinion. When he asked me how I felt, I said I was okay except for the odd headache, but although I didn't feel quite myself, I was sure it was nothing a few flying hours wouldn't cure, it was just the tonic I needed. He smiled at that and said the headaches may be cured by laying off the beer.

He wouldn't agree to resumed flying, he said that I had to take it easy for a while and report to him weekly, whilst he made enquiries in the UK through the Group to obtain my medical file from Rauceby and he would then, reassess my flying career as the position became clearer. In the meantime I would still receive flying pay.

Reporting the next day to the boss, he had the report on his desk and asked me how I felt. I said I wanted to fly, he said, 'Good man, the best thing for you is to get you airborne right away, but I can't ignore the MO's advice unfortunately. We have a full account of your prang now, you are exonerated from all responsibility, not that I for one ever doubted it. You may rest assured that I will get you airborne as soon as I am given the word, in the meantime make yourself acquainted with the Mark IX pilot's handbook.' I don't know if it was an admission on his part that I had no training on it, or a criticism.

The next day the CO called me into his office and said, 'I have the very job for you, I was wondering whom I could spare, and you have experience of ground control.' Somewhat mystified I said I would be fit within a week or so. 'Yes you will but I'm in a fix and I want your assistance.' I agreed to anything rather than loaf about. He told me he was putting me in charge of airfield ground control and I was to take charge of a fully equipped covered truck. I would be under the orders of the Chief Controller that the airfield now boasted of, located in the small watch tower.

I had to go to see him and be interrogated about rules and flying regulations and satisfy him I could do the job. There wasn't much to it really but it was something I knew a little about and it would be a new challenge. I had two airmen under me, one was supposed to drive the vehicle and the other to prepare and hand me the equipment and also listen to the radio. It didn't work out like that, I did the driving, it was more fun. I was mobile now, free to drive anywhere in the camp. The lads took the mickey out of me – but when I offered them lifts to the mess on the hill they gladly accepted. OK, I said, hang on while I find my ticket machine, it will cost you ten Kroner each; this is a private company now and the driver has to get his beer money from somewhere. Howls of ribaldry rent the air. I was nearly lynched, but I was in the driving seat. It was a good-natured way of getting my own back and they knew I didn't mean it. When I let them out, they demanded I pay them for the agony of being thrown from one side of the van to the other; they had flirted with death for the first time in their lives, they insisted. The Grand Prix season hasn't started yet, said Mike.

The duties were straightforward, obtaining the flying duties of all aircraft for the day and driving to the end of the runway in readiness for take-offs and remaining there until they returned, nobody could move an aircraft anywhere, take-off or land without my permission. Power indeed! All orders were confirmed by the chap in the tower of course, who took the can back if anything untoward happened. The aldis-lamps with coloured glass was used during the day and very-lights in inclement weather and in the evenings. Radio reception was very poor in the valley and could not be relied upon, hence the necessity for visual aids, although we were equipped for communication between aircraft, control tower and myself. The only snag was being on call, for visiting aircraft, so I kept the vehicle at the mess, instead of its rightful place in the transport section. How could I get a meal in comfort otherwise? Admittedly after a long evening, the truck was seen careering down the hill a little too fast for the bends!

On the airfield were unserviceable BF109s, FW190s gradually getting smaller as trophy hunters tore them to pieces. But the little two-seater Luftwaffe Storch spotter planes, with numerous light aircraft were in constant use and a damned nuisance. Usually flown by senior staff officers they tried to ignore the rules by taking off on the grass, across the runway, disregarding wind direction – these small aircraft could become airborne in a very short space – and they couldn't be bothered to taxi to the runway in the normal manner.

They created a needless hazard and one had to be alert to warn an incoming aircraft not to land. Someone found an old German three-wheeler van powered by a motor-cycle engine, so I had it painted black and white and used it to chase some of these unruly characters across the airfield to give them a piece of my mind. The control truck of course had to remain stationary at the runway, so this little thing became very valuable. It certainly shocked the light aircraft pilots when I came alongside them and blasted a Very light at them. The squadron pilots were delighted, in the officers' mess they overheard conversations and everybody was asking, 'Who the hell is this character charging about the airfield like a bloody knight in black and white armour, pooping off a pistol like a flipping bandit? He's a bloody menace.' Of course they knew they were in the wrong and it went no further. Gradually everyone conformed with the rules and life became mundane again.

September arrived and I was pronounced medically fit for flying duties. The boss entered me in the flight book for 'Familiarization on Type' and at last I took off for a recce of the district. It was good to be back in my element feeling confident once again. Soaring over the mountains and fiords in a deep blue sky was exhilarating.

Kjevic was a one runway airfield in the valley of three hills and the fiord, the prevailing wind was always from the fiord, so one took off over the fiord and landed in a steep approach between the surrounding hills. As I flew over the mountains and down the valleys the glorious splendour of the scenery made a deep and lasting impression, impossible to appreciate at ground level. Completing the sector recce, I felt I was back where I belonged, this aircraft flew like a bird. The landing was a little hairy on the limited runway, braking hard to stop short of the fiord. Taxying back to the apron, I got a tremendous cheer from the lads. The CO arrived and asked how it went. I said, OK, sir.

'Right sergeant, you are back on the strength.' Later that month I was promoted to flight sergeant.

As time went by I began to feel restless with the inactivity, flying for the sake of it was losing its appeal, the aircraft were not up to scratch and I did not have the same implicit faith in these Mark IXs as I did in our wartime Mark XIVs. They were ageing fast, they were far from new when we took possession of them after extensive operations and spare parts were at a premium. I had my old confidence back and threw them about the sky with the old aplomb, not-withstanding I had very few flying hours on them. But they were not dependable. The first of the Mark I ever flew, put me in hospital, and it wasn't easy to forget it. Nevertheless something else was missing from the scene, the adrenalin wasn't flowing, there was a distinct lack of excitement to keep one's skill attuned, to stay on the top line – no danger of being shot down. Of course I didn't relish the idea of an engine failure over this terrain but we always had sufficient height to bale out if necessary.

During the war one felt one was part of a team and doing fundamental work of paramount importance, in which one reached a peak of performance – this was no longer present. A certain amount of exasperation crept in making one inclined to be reckless when the aeroplane's performance wasn't up to scratch. It was a bad sign, but I don't think I was alone, judging by some hairy landings executed by others. One chap bought it attempting to land from an extremely tight turn on his approach at a low height from the down-wind leg – trying to save time. He was side-slipping in, stalled and went straight in. The aircraft exploded and there was no chance of saving him even if he was alive.

Air-sea rescue duties on the fiord were executed by the Norwegian Navy in British built Motor Torpedo Boats. They were excellent fellows, hard drinking, but real friends. Fortunately they were never called on, but members of the squadron were invited to sail with them on exercises, and if one liked travelling at 50 knots through the rough waters of the fiord, soaked with spray, it was a joy and a lifetime experience. The two boats were tied up at the Kjevic landing-stage, a 'cocktail' party aboard meant lying in a bunk, the despatching the refreshments as they were passed around the tiny cabin. There was no room for standing in any of the cabins, or wardroom. Problems arose on leaving, one had to climb the steep companionway, through a small hatch to reach the deck, then lever oneself into an upright position – this was a work of art. How they lived and worked aboard these all-engine boats was impossible to visualise. Naturally the squadron reciprocated inviting them to the squadron messes, but in much more comfort. It was very reassuring to have one's own rescue boat always at readiness, maybe a little under the weather, but extremely efficient at their work, both on and off the water, they rescued many a squadron member in their company on land, when they were faced with hostile Quisling type characters. There were no camp boundaries or gates, the local populace used the tracks through the woods on the hillsides to reach their destinations. The Navy Petty Officers were great friends of mine, we had an affinity from our first meeting, possibly because I showed more interest in their craft and liked to hear of their waterborne activities during the war. They all spoke English perfectly, making conversation a pleasure.

On one occasion I had the misfortune to buckle another Spitfire, I admit I probably didn't have my mind on the job but it wasn't all down to me. Coming in to land one day, I made the perfect approach to the runway, side-slipped in to lose height but I didn't keep my eye on the air-speed indicator. She was coming in too fast, but I thought everything would be ok to land and overshoot slightly as I saw the wind-sock ballooning out horizontally, indicating the wind was strong directly against me and should have slowed down the ground speed. I had done it before and the brakes worked perfectly. This time, not particularly worried, it was a good three-point landing. I pressed hard on the brake lever on the control column, ready for the aircraft to swing one way or the other using the rudder bar, but too late – a faulty pneumatic system wouldn't allow sufficient pressure to be brought to bear on the drums. There was nothing I could do but sit there and watch the end of the runway and the drop into the fiord looming nearer and nearer; there was no way of stopping and not enough runway left to take off again. I swerved but without power there was little response, so she dropped over the end ever so gently into the shallow water and broke her tail. I was okay except for a ducking.

Although I got a rousting from the CO for the short landing the whole matter was soon forgotten. Who needed Spitfires now, they were to be scrapped in their thousands anyway. Later on a visiting brass-hat in a Spitfire did exactly the same thing, to everyone's amusement.

The usual inquiry was held and dropped, just another accident due to brake-failure. I developed a very bad cold from the ducking, the water was freezing. But this led to complications with my ears and the new Medical Officer grounded me until it cleared up. He said he didn't want any perforated eardrums to explain away. Flight Lieutenant Morwood, the old MO, was posted away in September. One couldn't keep track of the changes of personnel around the place these days. Six pilots were sent home and replaced. However I convinced him I was fit again within a few days. I was bored stiff.

I resumed flying on 2 October carrying out exercises, formation flying, tail-chasing, aerobatics, and a cross-country trip to Folge Glacier with nine aircraft. The Glacier was well worth the trip, one mass of ice all the year round glinting in the rays of a weak sun was a fantastic sight. The most poignant recce was a flight to Telemark, where the German heavy water plant at Vemork near Rjukan became the target for British SOE (Special Operations Executive) and the Linge Company of the para-military partisan organisation Milorg. Winging through these beautiful valleys and over the inland lakes now so peaceful and tranquil, I flew over the spot where two Halifax tugs and their gliders carrying 50 British Commandos came to grief on the mountainside, in atrocious weather, on a previous attempt on the plant. The survivors from the crash were all shot. It was hard to visualise how much death and destruction had taken place in this rugged terrain. Back in the Low Countries and Germany the evidence was there for all to see.

Flying continued until the 12th when the squadron was notified that it was to move to Gardermoen to prepare for the flight back to England. The weather had worsened throughout September and into October. Many days were flightless and No 88 Group decided that Norway was to be evacuated before the onset of winter. Orders were that the aircraft had to be nursed to get them into serviceable trim for the long haul home. They were at the end of their days. No new Spitfire IXs had been built for years and they were at the stage where they were stuck together with chewing gum and string, figuratively speaking. They were, with the exception of a few, the same aircraft that had given the German armoured divisions a rough time in the last stages of the war, when they were equipped with 500lb bombs; over a year ago. Replacement Spitfires were secondhand aircraft and allowances had to be made for the lack of top-grade maintenance. Conversation with the ground crews brought out what was uppermost in everybody's minds, and that was, when were they going home. They were short-handed and under pressure servicing two squadrons and the maintenance suffered as a consequence. Despite this, the aircraft still had a magic of their own. They were always such a delight to fly when they were on song. They were incomparable.

XII

Au Revoir to the Service

On 13 October the squadron said goodbye to Kjevic as all Spitfires took off for the last time and headed north for Gardermoen (Oslo) where they were to be thoroughly overhauled before the journey home to the UK. More facilities were available at this base. Our servicing echelon were left behind to embark for home two days later. On arrival at Oslo we were in the hands of the ground crew servicing 176 Squadron and all unnecessary flying was forbidden; to conserve the aircraft. Weather permitting, air tests were carried out but no violent manoeuvres were allowed. The weather had turned very nasty with the onset of winter and for one period of four days no aircraft left the ground. In the meantime we were entertained by the city officials and ex-partisans with the luncheons and dinners. We received numerous gifts, I acquired a fur hat and leather mittens to go with the coat I had already received. From various bodies of business men I was given necklaces of semi-precious stones and a golden type of metal found in Norway, and a variety of odds and ends to suit lady friends. The most treasured gift I received was a pair of good quality fur-lined boots.

Some squadron pilots were sent home on leave about 24 October, I should have been one of them, but I was a sort of dogsbody and held back. A nucleus of pilots had already been formed for flying the squadron aircraft home later. Towards the end of the month 90-gallon slipper drop-tanks were fitted to the Spitfires for longer range. They had to be tested and formations of 18 aircraft flew to Kristiansand and back. On 2 November Flight Lieutenant Sibley, a favourite of us all (one of the old-timers), called out over the radio that he had engine failure and fell out of formation. The squadron was nearing the base and it was hoped he would make a forced landing. Flight Lieutenant Gibbins broke off to search for him, he found the wreckage and reported that from the appearance of the aircraft there could be no hope of the pilot's survival; he had gone straight in. It was all very sad for those of us who really knew him. He was with the squadron when I joined them in the hectic days of 1945. We thought he deserved a squadron of his own, but the end of hostilities probably robbed him of his promotion and his own command. His demise was deeply disturbing. Two days later and he would have been home on a well deserved leave, with no doubt, a promising future ahead of him whatever he turned to.

The morning of 3 November was a hive of activity. Only 17 aircraft were serviceable for the long journey home. I thought I was bound for home on the next transport out when someone was taken ill and I had to hurriedly prepare to take his place, not forgetting the mae west this time. All my baggage had gone to Turnhouse (Edinburgh) on a transport plane with the party that left earlier. Fortunately I was in my best uniform.

The squadron took off eventually just before lunch and formed up over Oslo and set course for Kastrup (Copenhagen); it was goodbye to Norway. The boss hugged the coast as much as possible, crossing the Skagerrak without incident and landed at Copenhagen about an hour-and-a-half later. The next leg was to be the longest to Manston (Kent) in the morning, so we relaxed and went out on the town to see the sights and take in the local colour. One couldn't let his hair down in view of the next day's trip, but we enjoyed the very short stay and retired to bed early. Some of the officers found a night-club and made merry, arriving back in the early hours of the morning.

After breakfast the following morning, the squadron took off, but were diverted to Hamburg (our old hunting ground of more than eighteen months ago) due to very bad weather over Bremen. This was directly in our path for home. However for some reason unbeknown to me, the CO decided that we would continue the flight after lunch. The cloud base at Hamburg was very low but we got airborne again and climbed through 10/10ths cloud to 25,000 feet into clear air, where the sections formed up on the leader and headed for Kent. With the assistance of air-traffic controllers through the Low Countries the squadron landed at Manston in time for tea.

We were directed to a dispersal on the fringe of the airfield, probably one that in the old days, was on the other side of a public road that ran through the airfield, and buses were a regular feature on it. In the early days of the war the airfield was extended and took in a public house, where regular clients sat and watched the fighters come and go from the dispersal situated in the car park, along the same road to the airfield. Of course after all the intervening years the pub and road had gone, it was one large airfield with runways now. During the Battle of Britain it took the full force of the Luftwaffe bombing attacks on the coast of Kent, and was wiped out more than once, squadrons had to be evacuated. Now it was all brand new, a typical peacetime RAF Station with all its attendant implications.

It wasn't long before my airmen colleagues became acquainted with the new regime; peacetime bull was entirely new to them, it was a foreign service. We were reported to the station adjutant on the very first day, tramping around between the living quarters and the sergeants' mess clad in flying gear. This was strictly *verboten*; high-necked white sweaters, scarves, flying boots, and flying jackets were only allowed during flying, never on the ground. It came as no surprise to me, but when we strolled into the sergeants' mess, ravenously hungry after our long trip horrified looks gave us the message and guess what? The station WO came in as we were sitting down to a meal and nearly blew a gasket when his searching eyes alighted upon us. He didn't know we had just arrived. In future he said, members of his mess will change from working clothing (as he called it) and dress properly before entering it. I had already sailed close to the wind in Norway, so I kept my mouth shut very firmly. The three warrant officers all decorated with the DFM didn't take too kindly to being admonished in this manner, especially Phil. They more or less told him to make himself scarce to put it politely, the meal was getting cold. The SWO cleared off muttering to himself.

The next day all the squadron was sent on a fortnight's leave. When I arrived back, there were a number of fighter squadrons on the station including 176 who were stationed at Gardenmoen when we were there. No-one knew what was happening, I found myself billeted with strangers and when I went out to the dispersal there were a number of new faces around. Some of our mob I never saw again, by that I mean of course 130 Squadron's NCO pilots. The spare pilots that left Oslo for Edinburgh were dispersed and I have no knowledge of their whereabouts, they may have been sent on leave or demobbed.

I missed my old room mate Mike Ockendon; he was sent on leave and I never saw him again. Somebody mentioned that he had been posted on an officer's course, but it was only a buzz. Manston was a busy station and nobody at the dispersal seemed to know what the form was.

A large exercise was mounted on 27 November, involving a mock battle with 12 Group fighters, and the squadron had a busy time. I was told I wasn't required and to keep out of the way, so I cleared off to the town alone feeling a bit miffed and got three sheets in the wind.

The CO called me into his office and told me that I was to be released from the service – I couldn't be discharged as I was a regular. He asked me what I intended to do in civilian life, I said on the spur of the moment that I had no idea. I hadn't given it any thought. The service was my life and I had lived it from day to day since joining the squadron. He told me he had to sign my release papers as the squadron would shortly move to Charterhall; he was signing them prematurely as my Commanding Officer, but I would be left behind at Manston to be processed. He recommended me as a proficient single-engined pilot, and as an experienced wireless/radio operator. He was in fact, only putting in writing my service qualifications. I had no civilian qualifications. My release took effect from 12 December 1945, but I was not discharged until the following March.

*

Berwick-on-Tweed had gone through the war as though it had never happened, nothing had altered in any way, the environment was as beautiful as ever, the people as morose. Not an enemy aircraft had been seen throughout the entire campaign and apart from rationing, it never felt the effects of wartime. The only people who saw something of it were the engine crews journeying between Newcastle and Edinburgh on the main line, but only at the terminals. They had a hard time of it father told me. In the black-out, signal lights were reduced to pin-points, no lights were allowed anywhere, the cabs were covered in to prevent light from the firebox showing which made the inside of the cab stiflingly hot. They drove with their heads out of the window most of the time, without any protection from the weather, or goggles for their eyes. Numerous accidents occurred in the marshalling yards to the shunters and staff with engines and trains moving about virtually blind. The traffic on the railway had increased tremendously due to the war of course and had I remained there, I would be a driver now. Such is fate.

The first thing I did was to rid myself of the demob suit – feeling guilty about giving it to the Salvation Army, who had done nothing to deserve the insult. Precisely what my future was I hadn't the remotest idea and at that time I didn't care. I couldn't see any in Berwick, so I set out to enjoy my new found freedom for a while, renewing old friendships with my old pals of school days and the teenage years; which seemed a lifetime ago.

Doing the rounds of the local hostelries every night couldn't go on for ever of course, money wasn't short, I spent very little on the continent, there was nothing to buy, and my credit mounted up to a huge sum for those days, plus the gratuity on leaving the RAF. I was a wealthy man comparatively speaking, so I decided to give myself a year to readjust to civilian life.

I was beginning to sort myself out when the squadron paid another visit, this time to Acklington. I walked into the late Rum Puncheon of happy memory one night, to find the place crawling with chaps in civilian clothing, but one couldn't mistake a few of the familiar faces immersed in pint beer glasses. They had found the place on my recommendation when they were at Charterhall and liked it so much they motored up for another visit. We had a wild night drinking and yarning about old times, I was disappointed to find only the latest arrivals among the NCOs, I understood that Phil, Mike and Micky had been discharged but they had applied for short-term commissions and would re-enter the RAF and train at an officers' college. There had been big changes in the flying personnel, and a lot of new faces, all officers, new sprog pilots straight from an OTU: a great occasion for 'line shooting'. As a civilian I was on level terms now with everyone and the new pilots who missed the war sat listening to us as we swapped anecdotes. It was the first time I ever had the pleasure of speaking to other pilots from the lofty heights of an experienced combat pilot.

The reunion bucked me up whilst it lasted but the next morning came reality. I was toying with the idea of rejoining the RAF, life at home was one long bore with nothing to do and I was making it unhappy for my parents also; we weren't compatible. But it was obvious from what the chaps told me, there was no future for me except in my old trade on the ground.

Helicopters, in their infancy then would have provided an ideal flying job for me, if there was nothing else, but once again the pilots were officers only. The new air force as my old CO had told me, didn't want senior NCO pilots any more in any branch of flying; they were redundant, but as Loadmasters for dropping in the drink on air-sea rescue duties they were ideal; it would appear that nothing had changed in that department in the new peacetime RAF. The pre-war system had reasserted itself regarding commissions. So that put an end to any further ideas of extending my service.

I joined Berwick Rowing Club for exercise and to fill time in, I was a singles sculler many years ago so I took to it like a duck out of water again, if the reader will excuse the pun. It suited my mood rowing alone and the Tweed was a lovely river on which to enjoy solitude. Shortly afterwards I met a certain young lady who changed my life. Her name was Kathleen, but to her many friends she was simply Kay. I must have bored her to death she was such a good listener. For the first time, I had met someone who was interested in me and my service life, so I poured my soul out to her. It did wonders for me psychologically, I had a new purpose in life. I was going to marry her although she didn't know it then. The depression left me and I was full of optimism about the future. I was on a new plane and the first thing I did was to get a job in the GPO as a Postal and Telegraph Officer in the Telegraph Dept, eventually taking charge within a few months. I regretted not meeting her earlier before I squandered most of my bank balance, but one can't have everything. Her vivacious personality attracted many friends and when we got engaged I was flying at 40,000 ft. Our friends threw a party in honour of the occasion and we all enjoyed a memorable evening. I thought I was extremely lucky to have won the day. She was well aware that the future was no sinecure, it was going to be hard work for both of us, but her strength of character and support saw us through the bad patches lying in wait.

The first bad news to upset the idyllic atmosphere was when I was informed by the Postmaster that the Telegraph department was to close down in the name of progress and as I was not yet a permanent civil servant I was made redundant. All telegrams were to be telephoned to the Newcastle regional office for onward transmission. Subscribers were automatically linked up to Newcastle when they asked for 'Telegrams'. I must be the first person to be made redundant in the country, a few months after I started.

However the Postmaster had taken a liking to me and told me that if I was prepared to move to Newcastle, he would contact the Head Postmaster there and recommend me for a post if there were any vacancies. I thanked him but didn't expect anything to come of it. Certainly if there was a vacancy I had no choice but to accept it, but I didn't know how Kay would react. It meant her giving up a good career at Berwick and leaving all her friends, she wasn't a native of the place but she had grown to love it after she was demobbed from the WRNS. Our wedding was to take place in Berwick of course, but this unexpected development threw our plans to the winds.

A letter arrived from Newcastle offering me the same post I had at Berwick with no loss of seniority if I accepted immediately and it would count towards a permanent staff position. The old Berwick Postmaster had been true to his word, I discovered later I had jumped the queue of local Newcastle applicants attending the GPO teleprinter school; he must have been a man of influence. I gratefully accepted.

Efforts to obtain a job as Air Traffic Controller with the Government had come to nought. Their reply to my letter was the most enigmatic, ludicrous document I've ever received. They said, 'The very fact that you were a fighter pilot shows that you haven't the characteristics to be trained as an efficient controller.' Quite what that meant was a mystery to me and has remained so ever since. Further correspondence didn't clarify the meaning behind those few words. Frankly I was of the opinion that the quick-witted coolness of a fighter pilot was the temperament required for such a post and I told them so in no uncertain terms. Correspondence ceased.

Kay agreed I should go to Newcastle and she would join me. Luckily her parents lived in the district, anywhere else and we would have had accommodation difficulties to add to our troubles. Kay would have loved to be married in her parish church where she had attended regularly until the war took her away, but the vicar wasn't cooperative or sympathetic, money and status was the key word. His attitude did nothing for his or my faith, and no-one was more upset than Kay who had more faith than any of us. He required too many time wasting formalities at huge financial expense. I was expected to start work at Newcastle as soon as possible. We skipped the formalities, married in the registry office and squeezed a honeymoon in.

I liked the huge Telegraph Room from the moment I saw it, similar in size to Air Ministry Signals employing about 80 people round the clock, receiving and sending telegrams to all parts of the country and the world, via a very fast teleprinter keyboard system. These machines had no visual copy, it took some getting used to, one typed out the telegram blindly and the message came out on a tape at the side of the receiver at the destination, so it was like typing on a dummy keyboard. If one made a mistake, one was unaware of it, unless a query was made at the other end. The whole thing was silent. 100 per cent accuracy was expected at 60 words a minute.

When Peter was born I found it hard to make ends meet financially. I had to volunteer to do permanent night duties which was a seven night week, in order to earn extra money. The only fault with the GPO was the poor salary, I was earning less than a third, of what I was paid for flying, and I had two more mouths to feed and no home of my own. When complaints were made about the salary, the authorities trotted out the same old cliché – we would receive a handsome free pension at the age of 60 when we retired.

A year or so later a rumour went around that the Telegraphs were closing down throughout the country, telegrams were to be faded out completely. The Postal & Telegraph Officers were to be re-employed in the brand new national DHSS Pensions. Well I was aghast with this news. To cut a long story short, I washed my hands of the Civil Service that weekend and started my new job with the Press Association.

XIII

Airborne Again

Life from then on improved on all fronts: domestically we could afford more, the work was easily within my capacity, and we made more friends. I had more time off, but owing to the nature of newspaper work much of it was taken up with the recompense of high financial reward. We moved to our own house, nothing much to shout about, but if it wasn't for my wife's resolute persistence, we wouldn't have had that. The local authorities were no help whatsoever. I was just another of the thousands of ex-servicemen left to fend for themselves.

More than anything, we wanted to possess our own house, with the odd hours I worked between 7am and 4pm the following morning I naturally worked shifts. I wasn't getting my proper sleep during the daytime when on nightshift due to the hubbub and noise of the neighbourhood. So I took on extra work at the *Daily Mirror* and *Daily Mail* local offices. It was very lucrative. On approaching the secretary of the PA tentatively asking for financial assistance, I was pleasantly surprised when the directors offered to advance me an interest free loan as part of a deposit to acquire our very own house on the outskirts of Gateshead.

One evening I breezed into the town headquarters and social club of No 607 (County of Durham) Squadron, Auxiliary Air Force, at Jesmond and introduced myself. I was looking for a story as it happened. 607 was a famous fighter squadron in the very early days of the war, their exploits are too numerous to record here but I did write an article about their history.

As it happened, their old CO was there and we got on chatting about the war and discovered we had a lot in common. I liked him immensely, he was so down to earth, so much akin to my old wartime CO but much older. He had led his squadron in the Burma campaign until they were disbanded out there. I gave him a resume of my career in the RAF and we had a few laughs as we swopped anecdotes. The advantage of civilians is that everyone is on the same level, and this conversation could never happen in the service. He invited me to be his guest, I was an interloper here and he insisted on buying all the drinks. He asked me if I had thought of flying again, they were short of experienced pilots on the squadron and he urged me to consider it. I said I would give it some thought, I had many commitments and as it was a spare-time squadron I wondered if I could find the time. I told him that I was tied up most weekends with my work and he realised that newspapers were a 24-hour 7-day a week industry, but he said I could fly at any time although weekends attracted most people to form a nucleus flight. They seldom flew a whole squadron together except for exercises when arrangements were made to have a full strength turnout. Regular RAF pilots sometimes made the numbers up for an exercise.

He said all that was necessary, was to drop in sometime with my flying log book and leave it with him, to have the details checked and verified. Once this formality was over, he and his officers would be glad to have me, especially as they had very few pilots that didn't require conversion. They were flying the Spitfire Mark XXII's – the last Spitfires to enter service – a slightly updated version of the old Mark XIVs of my wartime squadron, but they didn't come into operation before the end of the war. The Mark XXIs had too many faults and were quickly discarded – only one squadron ever possessed them in the last few months of the war. The Spitfire XIVs we flew were supposed to be a stop-gap until the XXIIs were built in numbers, but the XIVs proved far superior to any piston-engined fighters the enemy had, so the newer XXIIs were not needed and never came into operation until after the war. The £120 a year gratuity would be very useful he said, for getting back in my old element and doing something I knew I did best. He certainly had the gift of the blarney.

The whole idea appealed to me tremendously, once again I could experience the joys of flying and in a Spitfire of the latest design. It would be a private flying club in civilian life, without any discipline on the ground by the RAF. The squadron operated from RAF station Ouston with an RAF Officer Commanding; the only RAF personnel were a few ground staff for administrative purposes, kitchen staff and technical ground crews. They were supplemented by the auxiliary ground staff of the squadron when they attended, but the squadron was an independent unit on the station. This was the Royal Auxiliary Air Force, their contemporaries were of course – the Territorial Army.

A couple of weeks later, I called at Jesmond again with my log books, and left them in the care of the secretary, the old chap wasn't there. I spoke to a few curious officers at the bar and by their changed attitude when they realised I was not an ex-officer gave me doubts for the first time of whether I was doing the right thing. I felt I should retrieve the logs and clear off, but before I could do so the CO came in and greeted me with enthusiasm and the officers suddenly dropped their coolness.

I had the temerity to ask him if there was any chance of a commission, but instead of falling through the floor, he said I would have to apply to the Air Ministry. However, he advised that he had never known one to be granted in peacetime unless one was an ex-officer in the RAF. He also said my substantive rank of flight sergeant in the RAF would be reduced back to sergeant as a member of the RAuxAF and I would have to accept it if I signed on. 'But,' he said, 'don't let that deter you, rank is of no account here, you will enjoy yourself with us.'

I was summoned to Ouston a few weeks later where my logs were returned to me by a regular RAF flight lieutenant, who told me I had been accepted as a sergeant-pilot in the RAuxAF by the Air Ministry; no reflection upon me he said, but it was the normal procedure in the Auxiliaries to drop a rank. He didn't give any explanation why this was so.

Presumably it was the cut-price policy of the Air Ministry in peace-time in maintaining a reserve fighting force. Only the regular RAF staff who were full time, kept their rank from the time I left it.

This chap was the adjutant who looked after the squadron's affairs in their absence. He added that I had nothing to sign except a transference from the RAF Reserve to the Auxiliaries. I had forgotten I was still a reservist and could be recalled in the next three years.

Kay wasn't in favour of it, she thought I was doing enough, but the more I could earn the quicker we would have enough deposit to put down on a house and furnish it. I had no transport and I hadn't given it much thought, the airfield at Ouston was ten miles from home and five miles west of Newcastle, but fortunately I met a chap (F/Sgt Jack Bainbridge) who had a fast Ford V8 car who offered to give me a lift on Sunday mornings, when I was prevented by other commitments from attending on Saturday. One was expected to arrive on a Saturday, have a social evening at Chollerford Bridge Hotel a few miles up the old Roman Road and situated on the beautiful North Tyne. After staying overnight at the airfield, one put in as many flying hours as possible on Sunday, leaving for home in the evening. This wasn't convenient when my own work had to come first and many times I've had to climb out of bed and leave home at 6 am on a Sunday morning after working Saturday evenings, to walk the ten miles from home to the airfield, and reach it by 9 am – when Jack was unable to pick me up.

The Auxiliaries were upper crust types, and professional classes; very much so pre-war, when they were manned by the county class and some COs were peers and landed gentry. It seemed the only difference now was that they were replaced by accountants, solicitors, university graduates, etc. Leisure time was no obstacle, they could adjust their working hours to suit their commitments to the RAAF: putting me at a disadvantage from the beginning. They could drive out to the airfield and get some flying hours in at any time during the week, which was out of the question for me. In fact one didn't see much of the officers at weekends except in the pub on Saturday nights. There was still this division between officers and NCOs in this part-time outfit. A certain number of hours had to be flown every month to quality for the gratuity, consequently the weekend party included the three NCO pilots. Another problem arose when I discovered that the squadron was expected to take a fortnight off work for camping and exercises with the occupation forces in Germany at the height of the summer holidays. The CO had never mentioned this little matter.

When I informed our Centre chief (the manager) that I would be absent on exercises with the RAF, he had a fit. Firstly I had no right to join even the Boy Scouts without his permission he said, secondly he would on no account accommodate any arrangements I made with the squadron. I did point out that I was a reservist and the head office were well aware of the fact, but it cut no ice with him.

At that time, a fortnight was a whole year's holiday. With a small staff only one person could go at one time and a roster told one when it was his turn. There was no possible way my holidays were going to coincide with 607's camp, without his cooperation. To be honest I felt sure the firm would provide the time off to enable me to attend without using my family's holidays. They weren't expected to pay me for my absence, the Air Force compensated everyone for loss of work and with all expenses paid of course. The manager was adamant he was not going to lose my services for a fortnight and he refused to allow my appeal to the head office. If I had forced the issue I would have won, the Air Ministry would have been more than a match for him, he forgot I was still in the reserve and the Air Force could enforce him to comply with their wishes. The Fleet Street head office would have given permission, they were patriots, but it was more than I dared do to go over his head. However enough damage had been done, the atmosphere between him and myself cooled considerably. I had to cry off the first year's camp and of course our new squadron CO took a dim view of it. He had recently taken over from the old chap that talked me into joining the squadron. I hoped that the following year I would talk the boss into allowing me to go to camp, but it was now obvious relations were strained. I am sure he did not believe I was an ex-fighter pilot, or he didn't want to, when I made no mention of it on my application for the job. I was just an ex-serviceman. By his hostile attitude now he knew it was true, I wouldn't have got the job in the first place.

Missing the camp and manoeuvres lost me many flying hours. It showed when I received only £60 for my first year's work with the squadron. Many weekends in the winter were spent doing nothing due to the bad weather, but one received very little for that. One was paid according to the amount of flying hours one put in, consequently it was all a waste of time which could have been usefully spent at home.

Despite all these problems and obstacles, when I felt I just could not win, I enjoyed flying again. It was second nature, I was tested out on the old Harvard trainer of South African days and apart from refreshing myself with the cockpit layout and the various technical aspects of it, I had little difficulty in coming to terms with it after the halcyon days of the speedy Spitfire. I was glad to pick up where I left off and went solo one day on a cross-country exercise. I flew up to Berwick and beat up my old homestead, leaving I shook up the town by flying up the river under the two bridges, and through the arches, just for the devil of it. I wasn't looking for a summons, so I didn't hang about. With a waggle of wings to my parents I beat a hasty retreat westwards down on the deck, where the Radar station at Boulmer couldn't pick me up. I had committed the cardinal sin, I'm afraid. No doubt if my old squadron had still been at Charterhall, they would have given chase, but the airfield was empty now. What the hell did it matter now anyway. The greatest thrill any pilot enjoyed was low flying at speed. Some weeks later enquiries were made by the flight commander; a complaint had gone through the usual channels and taken time to reach Ouston. Fortunately other pilots had cross-country flights detailed to them that day and none of us admitted we had been anywhere near the Tweed and the matter was dropped.

Jack Bainbridge was one of the new age of pilots, joining the RAF too late to fly any operational aircraft, on discharge he immediately joined the Royal Auxiliary Air Force as a civilian and continued his flying with 607 Squadron which was disbanded in the Far East after VJ-day, and reformed after the war at Ouston with Spitfire Mark XIVs. He was unemployed, so he spent all his time at Ouston amassing a vast amount of flying hours on the light aircraft and Harvards. To him, it was his flying club and instead of paying for lessons, he was in fact earning a living from it. He quickly obtained his civilian flying licence and left the RAAF for a full-time commercial job with a small airline. The last I heard of him, he was flying with a foreign airline overseas. He was without doubt a very astute character and I took my hat off to him by using the service for his own ends. We became firm friends – with having to rely on him for transport I was dependent upon him – we messed together and in our free time when the weather prevented flying, we went on the binge together. His driving was hairy enough when he was sober, but after drinking he was a menace, we had a number of slight accidents on icy roads but never hit another vehicle – just the odd tree. Traffic was light on those country roads.

Of course there was an immense difference between us when it came to flying, stooging around merely flying an aircraft for the fun of it, had no comparison to using the aircraft as a fighting platform. Personally whilst I still liked throwing the aircraft around the sky, there was no motivation anymore, it was pretty tame in the training Flight, nothing but retraining exercises mostly in the old Harvard because of the shortage of serviceable Spitfires. I complained that I was being held back from the operational section, I was being out-ranked by the senior pilots and couldn't get out of the Training Flight. This didn't go down too well with the Flight Commander, who said I hadn't flown sufficient hours with them.

Skimming over the beaches at Whitley Bay and Tynemouth at nought feet and scaring the daylights out of the holiday-makers was the only thrill left. However, keeping my nose clean, I was looking forward to a bigger challenge in the shape of the new Vampire jet fighters with which the squadron were re-equipping and working up on, but unforeseen natural causes decreed it wasn't to be.

I began to suffer with sinusitis, I couldn't depressurize my eardrums when descending from a great height to ground level, the pain was excruciating, and I had to climb again to relieve it. Attaining height, I gradually lost it in stages to balance the pressure inside the eardrum. A slight head-cold and aerobatics, particularly steep dives to reach sufficient speed in a Harvard, to execute a loop was all that was required to give me an attack. Not necessary in the Spitfire of course with their power but it was obvious that operationally I couldn't continue flying. It was brought home to me when I tried to sit a Harvard down on the runway and I was still 10 feet off the ground! Fortunately I had a co-pilot in the back seat who grabbed the controls and saved us both from a nasty accident. He was furious, he happened to be with me because he couldn't find a spare aircraft of his own. If he hadn't taken control she would have flicked over on her back in the stall and crashed upside-down on the runway. It goes without saying, I would never have written this document.

I had to report it and was sent to the squadron's civilian doctor, who was a right pain in the backside – he said I had tuberculosis! He said he would have me X-rayed. Filled with alarm I went to see my own doctor, who was so annoyed he phoned this character in my presence and told him he was a fool to tell his patient he had an unfounded illness, and I wouldn't be happy now until it was proven. My doctor sent me immediately for an X-ray to put my mind at ease. I sent the doctor's note to the squadron adjutant, what transpired I don't know, I was requested to attend a medical board at RAF Thornaby some time later. When I arrived at Thornaby they had gone, no-one knew anything about me; a wasted journey. No correspondence came from the squadron, my discharge papers declaring me unfit for service arrived by post from the A.M. some time later.

After 18 months with them, it was goodbye to flying for ever. I can't say I regretted leaving 607. The old CO who talked me into joining them was as outdated as I was, he lived in the past and would not have fitted in with this present outfit either; they weren't an integral unit and team spirit was nil. They were a strange mixture of pilots, none of them had flown with 607 at any time during the war, and they had flown a variety of aircraft.

On the credit side we bought a lovely house due to the considerably increased financial position. It was a new world to us. Kay worked part-time and Peter went to a new school.

For many years the work was exciting, we were also sent on outside assignments. When the Prime Minister of the day, Mr Harold Wilson toured the north and other well-known politicians of different persuasions visited the district, I assisted the chief reporter in giving them countrywide news coverage, other work involved covering sports events and more to my heart, I was a specialist railway correspondent for the PA. My early training and youthful experience of the old London & North Eastern Railway which I maintained throughout my life was invaluable. Besides keeping in touch with the RAF I became a railway historian, keeping abreast of the latest developments. The day to day work became humdrum and I was always looking out for the unusual and sometimes got on the team that covered the Assizes where some very notorious murder and night club conspiracy cases were heard.

In later years I began to suffer from prolapsed disc trouble and had to put comfort first, particularly the seating. This handicap increased with time and led to me being incapable of work, firstly in weeks, then over some months and finally I was incapacitated for two years. My condition worsened and it was – according to a consultant and my own ex-military doctor – the manifestation of an injury sustained in the crash-landing in Lincolnshire, May 1945, which was not apparent at the time. I had to cease part-time work for other newspapers as the injury worsened.

After various forms of treatment, I was adjudged incurable, a registered disabled person, nothing more could be done, the RAF disclaimed all responsibility after 40 years and I was unable to claim a war pension. I tried to continue my work but found it impossible, I had to retire. My employers appreciated the position and we came to an amicable financial arrangement. I was with the Press Association for 33 years.

Despite my disablement, I have to think myself lucky to survive the war and able to give loyal service to my civilian firm for more than three decades before my health failed me – a life that so many other comrades never had the chance of fulfilling. Although I did not take part in the early years of the Battle of Britain, I feel that I am one of the few, in as much as I am one of the few fighter pilots, who survived throughout the whole war, and in particular, one of the exceedingly few non-commissioned officers of the Royal Air Force.

Epilogue

Looking back over the years, I made some foolish mistakes in my career that can only be put down to ignorance and lack of foresight. My zealous, aggressive attitude stood me in good stead. Without it, I would have achieved nothing whatsoever: on the other hand it was my worst enemy. In 1938 I was in between two stools, my life had been devoted to locomotive engineering when it suddenly came to a halt. Accepting the new challenge and orientation of service life in the RAF of which I had no previous knowledge, changed my whole outlook on the world at large. Academically I knew how to fly an aeroplane and I hoped one day I would be given the chance to prove it. I know now that if the war hadn't commenced this would never have happened. After seven years' service I would have been discarded without a trade to my name, and extremely lucky if I attained the great heights of the rank of corporal as a General Duties Aircrafthand at the end of it.

In fact I was certain to become one of the disciplinary HQ section that I learned to heartily despise. Then I would have been thrown on the street as nothing more than a labourer, or wasted the rest of my life in extended service, always assuming of course the RAF still required my services. Part of the appeal of the RAF was the glamorous overseas service – I unashamedly admit I was a romantic supporter of the British Empire – nothing gave me more pleasure than to read of the far-flung outposts of the Air Force and their operations against unruly Arabs in Mesopotamia – from Turkey, Lebanon, Iraq, and Syria to Bahrein – Palestine, Egypt, Sudan, Afghanistan, the North-West Frontier, India and the Far East were magical names when I was a schoolboy. I hoped I would reach some of these parts or anywhere else in the world as a responsible member of the RAF with a trade to my name.

Then came the war a year later, the auxiliaries and the volunteer reserve were mobilized, and the mad scramble of eligible young men to get into the RAF rather than wait to be called up and find themselves soliders and sailors without any choice in the matter. These civilians were trained as tradesmen, over our heads and denied the regular airman of such advancement. Naturally the regulars were bubbling over with excitement in September 1939, anticipating a surge in training and advancement, after all, those serving in all the armed forces were expected to take the brunt of the fighting from the onset of war. The general public were no doubt eager to do their bit for the country but the serving forces were more so. They expected the new men to take a back seat especially in the RAF. It was a dreadful disappointment to those of us in the General Duties branch not to be given any opportunity, when the war was imminent, to improve our lot. The lack of foresight by the governing bodies of the RAF was criminal – anyone who could read and write, would undoubtedly pass now – standards were considerably reduced to accommodate the new wartime intakes. We regular chaps were not allowed to sit further examinations with them in competition and test educational and intellectual abilities for the new aircrew and ground trades which were to expand at a rapid rate. It took six years to prove there were people like me, already in the service, who were capable of flying an aeroplane as efficiently as an officer.

With one's post-war future uppermost in one's mind, anyone who opted to fly fighters was a fool, but the vast majority of this body of men never considered the aftermath, fortunately for the country. They had no future in the air as civilians. I realised too late in the day, civilian airlines were only interested in multi-engined bomber pilots and it would appear, that the government air controllers department were of the same opinion. A foolish mistake on my part, because I could not capitalize on being a fighter pilot unless I became a national hero with a string of decorations and the ability to inveigle the press and the public into reading of my prowess – with the aid of well-kept diaries, ghost writers and profit making publishers. Having said that, my ambition to be a fighter pilot and to fly the Spitfire overrode any injustice of the day and what the future had to offer to the likes of me when it all ended, assuming I was still around. I was just one of hundreds if not thousands of servicemen of all branches of the armed forces that were promptly forgotten by the Government as soon as their services were no longer required. But the regular serving men got the worst deal when no schemes were instituted to fit them for a life in civilian street. The reservists and conscripts had a good pre-war job to return to or to carry on their interrupted university studies as under-graduates. Those who died, lived for the day, under the impression that they were fighting for a better future for their country, but only the survivors know the truth.

The handicap of not being commissioned was apparent throughout my service career, but it was one of those things one had to bear, disregard it, and get on with the job in hand. Yes, I volunteered as a young man with zest and enthusiasm to prove I could fly and fight, and fought the establishment in order to do so – a bigger obstacle than the enemy.

Therefore some people would say I had no complaint. I always accepted that, but I never accepted the discrimination of rank although I was forced to be philosophical about it. It did not matter when one was doing his job in the air, but at any other time it certainly did. In post-war years it still carried influence as I discovered to my cost, the more senior the officer became the more gongs he was likely to attract as a matter of course. Like a magnet to pins: deservedly or not. Few airmen were decorated and to gain two decorations was extremely rare. The only difference was the recipient's status in rank. So what chance did an undecorated airman pilot have in the brave new world of Mr Churchill.

Today, I feel proud to have achieved the peak even though it was late in the day, despite the obstacles; my only regret is that I had to fight, not against the enemy, but against the bureaucracy of the RAF before being allowed to assert myself and coming to grips with them. As a consequence most of my service life was wasted. It was ludicrous that a chap with tin legs could sweep all before him, not that he wasn't worthy of all the admiration and honours bestowed upon him. On the contrary, he was without doubt a very courageous man. He knew the right people otherwise he would never have flown again, and what would it have done for his own mental stability if he had been refused. It wasn't on though when other fit men were denied this privilege and the subsequent advantages. I have learned the lesson albeit too late, that in this life, it was never a question of what one knew, it was always a case of *who* one knew. Social standing even in 1939 was more important than defeating the Germans, and remained so throughout the war and is still paramount in the structure of all the armed forces and the ruling bodies, whatever their persuasion. In no way was I ever prejudiced against RAF officers as a body of men, the vast majority were ordinary chaps like me. Except for the old boys' Alma Mater syndrome, officers thought the division between us was divisory and ludicrous, not to mention the difference in salary for doing the same work.

However on the brighter side, my life only started when I was called to report for aircrew training at Abbey Lodge early in 1943. The ground training in this country: the two voyages to the southern hemisphere; the flying training in the Union of South Africa and Egypt; were the most wonderful days of my life. These events could never have happened to me in the ordinary course of service life. I am indeed grateful to whoever was instrumental in placing them in my path, I would never have experienced the most happy, carefree, and fruitful 22 months that any one could possibly envisage in any other circumstances – culminating in the ecstatic realisation of a dream. Admittedly one had to pay the piper later, but it was worth every single day.

The sound of a Rolls Royce engine bursting into life with its unmistakable accompanying sound and smell as one sat behind it, and the excitement it generated to keep one's adrenalin flowing was worth more than any amount of money could buy, even a commission – it can never be forgotten.

Who could resist the appeal of that magical aeroplane whatever the outcome: the incomparable Supermarine Spitfire?

Index